MARX-ENGELS DICTIONARY

MARX-ENGELS DICTIONARY

James Russell

GREENWOOD PRESS

WESTPORT, CONNECTICUT

Library of Congress Cataloging in Publication Data

Russell, James, 1944-
 Marx-Engels dictionary.

 Bibliography: p.
 Includes index.
 1. Communism—Dictionaries. I. Title.
HX17.R87   335.4'03'21   80-786
ISBN 0-313-22035-2 (lib. bdg.)

Library of Congress Catalog Card Number: 80-786
ISBN: 0-313-22035-2

First published in 1980

Greenwood Press
A division of Congressional Information Service, Inc.
88 Post Road West, Westport, Connecticut 06881

Printed in the United States of America

10 9 8 7 6 5 4 3 2 1

COPYRIGHT ACKNOWLEDGMENTS

To
Hans H. Gerth   1909–1978

Teacher of generations of radicals, refugee from fascism,
and example of intellectual integrity always.

CONTENTS

CONTENTS

CONTENTS

ACKNOWLEDGMENTS

Over the years while this manuscript was taking shape, a number of people helped directly and indirectly. James O'Connor helped very early on with my understanding of some of the key Marxian economic concepts. Rob Kennedy and Anne Griffiths read later drafts and offered valuable suggestions. Finally, students in my classes at San Francisco State University and the Liberation School in San Francisco were the sharpest critics of the development of my clarity on these subjects. None of those who helped, of course, are responsible for any remaining errors or confusions.

INTRODUCTION

The social movements of the 1960s in Western Europe and the United States stimulated a renaissance of serious study of Marx and Engels. Many hoped to develop a deeper understanding of the causes of the movements which brought them to political activism. If the 1960s activism was an awakening, the study of Marx is the act of political maturing.

THE PROBLEM

But, the Marxian classics are not easily understood, as generations of frustrated activists, scholars, and general readers have discovered. Part of the difficulty is terminological and that is the motivation for this dictionary. The causes for terminological difficulties are many. The first is simply time. Many of Marx's and Engels's terms have gone out of general use or have acquired a different meaning in the hundred or more years since they appeared. This problem is encountered in reading any text from another historical period. The second is ideological in the sense of the sociology of knowledge. The Marxian conceptual apparatus represents a point of view that was and continues to be radically different from the prevailing bourgeois mode of thought. It is a terminology designed to represent not the ideas of a ruling class but rather the antithesis of those ideas, that is the historical point of view of the working class. Marx and Engels stated that the ruling ideas of an age are the ideas of the ruling class. It follows that it is difficult for any member of a capitalist society to break out of the bourgeois modes of thought, to see society conceptually as did Marx. The third cause is scientific. Marx and Engels took the best currents of Western economic, political, and philosophic theory to produce a qualitatively new synthesis. The concepts of the new synthesis were just that—new. Hence Engels warned readers of *Capital:* "There is, however, one difficulty we could not spare the reader: the use of certain terms in a sense different from what they have, not only in common life, but in ordinary Political Economy. But this was unavoidable. Every new aspect of a science involves a revolution in the technical terms of that science."

In addition to the problems of terms that were common only in the nineteenth century (for example, joint-stock company) or that have a particular Marxian meaning (for example, surplus value), the general reader is likely to have trouble with technical historical, economic, and philosophical terms (such as Zadruga, amortization, and monism). For all these types of problems ordinary dictionaries are of little use; the specialized Marxian use of the terms requires a correspondingly specialized dictionary.

CONCEPT CLARIFICATION

If access to the Marxist classics requires a familiarity with its terminology, the furtherance of Marxism as a science requires continual attention to concept clarification. Any science that strives for cumulative development must sharpen the accepted understandings of its basic concepts. Otherwise, to the extent that the basic tenets of the science are individualistically interpreted, that part of the cumulative development that is the result of the advantages of being a collective endeavor suffers.

This is not to argue for a dogmatic interpretation of the basics of Marxism. On the contrary, Marxism is a method for interpreting and changing the world, not a set of dogmatic assertions handed down *ex cathedra*. But attentiveness to method includes attentiveness to concept clarification. There can be a thin line between concept clarification and the idealist fallacy of fetishistically treating the definitions as more important than that which they define. Marxism constructs definitions in order to reflect the essence of a changing reality; as such, the definitions are secondary to that reality.[1] Though secondary, definitions are essential: revolutionary class consciousness is precisely the ability to define human and class reality accurately.

To expect everyone to agree with all the definitions would be totally unrealistic. No one could produce such a dictionary. Marxism is not positivism. There is plenty of room for disagreement on the fundamentals as the proliferation of tendencies within Marxism testifies. Thus one tendency or another will undoubtedly raise a howl of protests at the definition of particular concepts and will see the dark machinations of another tendency at work. There is nothing so calculated in this project. Although I have my own political perspective, my objective has been to come as close as possible to an orthodox Marxian rendition: to uncover what Marx and Engels meant by the terms in their writings. On some terms it is fairly obvious what they meant, but on others, interpretation must enter the definition. In those latter cases the reader will have to decide how reasonable the interpretation is.

With the exception of some post-Marx terms (such as historical materialism) that are widely used, only the terms that are in the writings of

Marx and Engels are included. Where available I have supplied definitions given by Marx and Engels. Where they used a term but did not define it directly, a derived definition appears. All the terms are in alphabetical order. Where advisable for the sake of clarity, I have grouped several terms under one heading (for example, *differential and absolute ground rent* under the heading *ground rent*). However, all terms are listed alphabetically in the table of contents though some may direct the reader to another heading.

NOTE   1. Cf. Proudon "has not perceived that economic categories are only abstract expressions of . . . actual relations and only remain true while these relations exist . . . the political-economic categories (are) abstract expressions of the real, transitory, historic social relations." Marx, letter to P. V. Annenkov, December 28, 1946.

MARX-ENGELS
DICTIONARY

A

Absolute and Relative Surplus Value: Two types of surplus value based on different strategies for increasing their production. Absolute surplus value is surplus value created by lengthening the time spent working. The production of absolute surplus value was an important early stage in capitalist development when the working day was increased in comparison with the working day of feudalism. Relative surplus value is surplus value created by making the worker more productive during the same unit of time. This is the major means of increasing surplus value production after the earliest stages of capitalist development. (See Marx, *Capital*, parts 3 and 4.)
See also SURPLUS VALUE.

Absolute Ground Rent. *See* GROUND RENT.

Absolutism: The type of state system in several European countries between the fifteenth- and eighteenth centuries (especially in England and France) where centralized power was disproportionately vested in a monarch at the expense of other state organs, such as a parliament. In the feudal period proper, the powers of the monarch were greatly limited by those of the local nobles. However, the rising bourgeoisie in the later stages of feudalism contested as a class the power of the nobles that had thwarted capitalist economic development. The rising bourgeoisie, in time, supported the establishment of an absolute monarchy as a way of weakening the stranglehold of the nobility over the economy. Engels interpreted the absolute monarchy as an exceptional form where the state was not controlled by any one class but rather was relatively independent. "Periods occur in which the warring classes balance each other so nearly that the state power, as ostensible mediator, acquires, for the moment, a certain degree of independence of both. Such was the absolute monarchy of the seventeenth and eighteenth centuries, which held the balance between the nobility and the class of burghers. . . ." (Engels, *The Origin of the Family, Private Property, and the State*, p. 168).

Abstract Labor. *See* CONCRETE AND ABSTRACT LABOR.

Abstraction: An intellectual construct that describes what is essential in an object of investigation by eliminating incidental or accidental features. The use of abstractions in analysis is a methodological device to break with superficial modes of thought. "In the analysis of economic forms, moreover, neither microscopes nor chemical reagents are of use. The force of abstraction must replace both." (Marx, "Preface" to the first German edition of *Capital*, p. 19.) The Marxist meaning of abstract thus differs from the popular meaning in which the adjective describes a vague idea or proposal. In art, abstraction has a parallel meaning to the Marxist. There, an abstraction is a created image that departs from a literal or naturalistic portrayal, often with the purpose of highlighting the essential.

See also CONCEPT; DEFINITION; DIALECTICS; and ESSENCE AND APPEARANCE.

Accumulation of Capital: *Economically*, the central goal in the capitalist mode of production ("Accumulate, accumulate! That is Moses and the prophets!"—Marx, *Capital*, p. 558). Surplus value, which has been produced in a production process, consists of two parts: *revenue* or the surplus value that will be individually consumed by the capitalist for food, housing, luxuries, and so on, and *capital* or the surplus value which will be reinvested in production. Hence, "employing surplus-value as capital, reconverting it into capital, is called accumulation of capital" (ibid., p. 543). *Historically*, the dynamic of the economic accumulation of capital unfolds in three general stages in the capitalist mode of production with a fourth consequence. Common to all the stages is that the accumulation of capital can only expand by progressively eliminating individual ownership of the means of production. First is the primitive accumulation of capital. The laborer's means of production are separated from her or him and capitalized, or transformed from her or his own means of production to means of production owned by another which now confronts the laborer as an alien force. A contradiction now exists between the laborer and her or his means of production.

> *The primitive accumulation of capital* includes the centralization of the conditions of labor. It means that the conditions of labor acquire an independent existence in relation to the worker and to labor itself. This historical act is the historical genesis of capital, the *historical* process of separation which transforms the conditions of labor into capital and labor into wage-labor. This provides the basis for capitalist production." [Marx, *Theories of Surplus Value*, part 3, pp. 314-15]

Second, accumulation of capital now is established by the continual reproduction on a larger and larger scale of the separation of laborers from the means of production. That is, the means of production in a society become capital—not the individual property of the laborers. *"Accumulation of capital* on the basis of capital itself, and therefore also on the basis of the relationship of capital and wage-labor, reproduces the separation and the independent existence of material wealth as against labor on an ever increasing scale" (ibid., part 3, pp. 314-15). Third, the concentration and centralization of capital. The capitalized means of production are fused together into larger units; that is, they become concentrated as opposed to scattered about the countryside. "Not an increase in *absolute* terms is presupposed, but *concentration*, the gathering together of more at a given point, and of *relatively* more [means of labor] compared with the number of workers brought together there" (ibid., p. 271). Centralization occurs when competition forces the merger or takeover of one capitalist enterprise by another. Capitalists expropriate capitalists; monopolization proceeds. Accumulation now has reached a level where the individual capitalists have neither sole ownership nor direct responsibility for the daily operation of individual corporations. They become superfluous to actual production.

> As *functionaries* of the process which at the same time accelerates this *social* production and thereby also the development of the productive forces, the capitalists become superfluous in the measure that they, on behalf of society, enjoy the unsufruct and that they become overbearing as *owners* of this social wealth and *commanders* of social labor. Their position is similar to that of the feudal lords whose exactions in the measure that their *services* become superfluous with the rise of bourgeois society, became mere outdated and inappropriate privileges and who therefore rushed headlong to destruction. [Ibid., p. 315]

Fourth, the stage is set for the resolution of the contradiction between labor and the means of production as capital. Labor is reunited with the means of production except now on a higher level, since in precapitalist times individual labor was united with the individualized means of production. Now social cooperative labor is united with socialized means of production.

See also CAPITAL; CONCENTRATION OF CAPITAL; CENTRALIZATION OF CAPITAL; PRIMITIVE ACCUMULATION OF CAPITAL; GOAL OF CAPITALISM.

Agnosticism: From the Greek "a" (negation) and "gnostics" (capable of knowing), meaning incapable of knowing. In religion, agnosticism takes the form of the belief that human beings do not have the faculty to ascertain whether a Supreme Being exists. In philosophy, agnosticism takes the form of Kantianism and neo-Kantianism, that is, the doctrine that humans are incapable of perceiving the true essence of life—the "thing in itself"—but only how the essence appears to us through the forms

internal to the mind. Marxists counter agnoticism by stating that science is capable of increasing the knowledge of essence.
See also KANTIANISM and NEO-KANTIANISM.

Alienation: The separation of one or more humanly defining conditions from human beings. Marx specified two humanly defining conditions of human nature: humans are *social* beings, and they develop their societies and themselves through *creative* labor. Since all class societies put individuals at war with one another, there is *ipso facto* alienation in the first sense—humans are separated from one another and hence from their social being. In the second sense of creative labor, there is structured alienation in all capitalist societies because workers are separated from control over a vital condition of their creative labor, the means of production. The capitalist class owns and controls the means of production. Hence workers are separated (alienated) from control over how their work is planned, how the product is to be used, their interrelationships with other workers, and lastly themselves, since the capitalist directs them instead of allowing them to be creatively self-directed.

Amortization: Technical economic term for the depreciation of value or wear and tear on the instruments of production. The root meaning of the word is from the French *amortir* or "to bring to death." As a machine is used in production, it gradually wears out, or goes *to death*, so to speak. In figuring the cost of production the capitalist "amortizes" the machine by calculating a percentage of its value which is equivalent to the amount of depreciation and averages this sum over the number of products produced in that time.

Anarchism: Non-Marxist tendency in radical political thought that views the state authority as the primary cause of social misery and therefore proposes its abolition as the road to social liberation. The primary proponent of anarchism in Marx's and Engels's time was the Russian Mikhail Bakunin (1814-1876). Marx and Engels opposed the anarchist program on the grounds that a strong workers' state would be necessary during socialism as a protection against counterrevolution and to pave the way for communism.
See also DICTATORSHIP OF THE PROLETARIAT.

Anarchy of Capitalist Production: Descriptive term for the causes and consequences of an economy that lacks centralized social planning. Private ownership of the means of production and competition preclude social and economic central planning in capitalist societies. One of the consequences is periodic economic crisis as well as continual social crises.

Ancient Society. *See* SLAVE SOCIETIES-ANCIENT SOCIETY.

Antagonistic Contradiction. *See* CONTRADICTION.

Antinomy: Kantian concept for unresolvable conflicts, contradictions, and problems in a system of thought.

Antithesis. *See* THESIS-ANTITHESIS-SYNTHESIS.

Appearance. *See* ESSENCE AND APPEARANCE.

Apprentice: In the feudal shop, a laborer who was serving a set period of on-the-job training in order to learn a craft or trade under the direction of a master.
See also FEUDALISM; GUILD; JOURNEYMAN; MASTER.

Appropriation: To take into one's own possession what was formerly not one's own. For example, the capitalist "appropriates" the unpaid labor of the worker in the production process.
See also PRIVATE APPROPRIATION.

A Priorism: Adherence to the *a priori* method in philosophy. *A priori* (Latin) means literally prior to experience whereas its polar concept, *a posteriori* means after or as a result of experience. *A priori* knowledge results from pure thought or reason unmixed with experience. In Kantian philosophy it is believed that the categories that mold thought and knowledge exist as pure and universal entities prior to experience. Engels described the *a priori* method as "ascertaining the properties of an object, by logical deduction from the concept of the object, instead of from the object itself" (*Anti-Duhring*, p. 116). Marx and Engels rejected *a priorism* for the materialist premise that experience is the starting point of knowledge.
See also MATERIALISM; HISTORICAL MATERIALISM.

Aristocracy: Political term from the Greek meaning "government by the best." In feudalism, aristocracy meant government by the people of highest social status as contrasted with, say, democracy which is government by all of the people regardless of social status. In the majority of cases in medieval Europe the aristocrats were the nobility. The term aristocrat also is used often as a designation for the status consciousness of the large landowners in the early period of capitalist development, especially in England.
See also NOBILITY.

Asceticism: The doctrine that knowledge and self-improvement are enhanced by self-denial of particular bodily comforts such as rich food, elaborate clothing, housing, warmth, or sex.

Asiatic Mode of Production: Pre-capitalist mode of production with the following characteristics: (1) The major division in society was between the state apparatus and agricultural villages. (2) The state taxed and absorbed the economic surplus of the villages for two main reasons—to finance infrastructural investments for the whole society e.g. irrigation projects, flood control, and roads, and for its own luxury consumption needs. (3) Each village possessed the land in common and communally shared the produce. Marx cited as examples of the Asiatic mode of production, "the Slavonic communes, in the Rumanian . . . in Mexico, Peru especially, among the early Celts, a few clans of India. . . ." (*Grundrisse*, p. 473).

Atheism: Worldview characterized by the absence of an appeal to the existence of a deity or deities to explain worldly reality.

Auxiliary Materials: One of the three parts of the means of production —the other two are the instruments of production and raw materials. Marx defined auxiliary materials as follows:

> Auxiliary materials are either means of consumption for machinery—in this case either fuel for the prime mover, or means of reducing the friction of the operating machinery, such as tallow, soap, oil, etc.—or they are auxiliary materials for buildings, like cement, etc. Or they are auxiliary materials for carrying on the production process in general, such as lighting, heating, etc. (in this case they are auxiliary materials required by the laborers themselves to enable them to work). Or they are auxiliary materials which enter into the formation of the raw materials as do all types of fertilizers and all chemical products consumed by the raw materials. Or they are auxiliary materials which enter into the finished product—coloring matter, polishing materials, and so on. [Marx, *Theories of Surplus Value*, part 1, p. 247]

Average Rate of Profit. *See* GENERAL RATE OF PROFIT.

B

Bank Note: A promissory note issued by a bank which can be exchanged by the bearer for a specified quantity of cash. "A bank-note is nothing but a draft upon a banker, payable at any time to the bearer, and given by the banker in place of private drafts" (Marx, *Capital*, vol. 3, p. 403).

Barbarism: Term used by Lewis H. Morgan, the nineteenth-century American anthropologist whose work influenced Engels's theory of the development of the family. After the descent of humans from the animal kingdom came a period of savagery and then a period of barbarism. Barbarism was "the period in which knowledge of cattle breeding and land cultivation was acquired, in which methods of increasing the productivity of nature through human activity were learnt" (Engels, *The Origin of the Family, Private Property, and the State*, p. 29). In other words, during barbarism humans began to produce as opposed to simply gathering the means for their survival.

Barter: Form of commerce where commodities are directly traded for each other without being transformed into money first.

Being: A concept with a long history in philosophy. The Greek Eleatic philosophers, especially Parmenides, asserted that True Being is the essence of things. That which is the essence is that which is common to all, that is, a universal property. Finding the universal, according to the Eleatic method, required a method of progressive abstraction. Hence, what is common between, for example, all pieces of paper is their "paperness." "Paperness" is not a tangible quality, rather, it is an idea. A step further in abstraction is that what is common between paper and all other things is their "isness" or true being. Note that "to be" is the infinitive of "is." Note also that true being is not tangible; it is an idea. The Eleatics were thus idealists because the essence of things, their being, was asserted to be an idea. Later philosophy struggled with the problem and added the categories of Nonbeing and Becoming. Hegel concluded that Being contains Nonbeing as its antithesis and the result of the

contradiction, the synthesis, is Becoming. Marx and Engels as material-
ists rejected the Eleatic conclusion that the essence of things, true being,
was an idea. They also rejected Hegel's dialectical modification of
Eleatic idealism, that true being as an idea contained its own negation,
nonbeing, and that the result of the contradiction—the synthesis or
negation of the negation—would be Becoming. Marx and Engels founded
their philosophical definition of being on a humanistic and materialistic
basis: ''. . . the being of men is their actual life-process'' (*The German
Ideology*, p. 42). In philosophy, true being and true universal are synonyms. Being in this sense is equivalent to totality.
See also TOTALITY; INDIVIDUAL, PARTICULAR, UNIVERSAL.

Benefice: Feudal legal concept for a grant of land conferred by a king
upon a subject in return for a specified obligation, usually military
service.

Bill of Exchange: Nineteenth-century term for a written promise to pay
for a loan, given by the debtor to the creditor. These bills of exchange
in turn could circulate on the money market, i.e. be bought and sold and
discounted in other transactions.

Bonapartism: The ideology and practice that corresponded to the Bona-
partist state which was one of the three types of capitalist state forms
analyzed by Marx and Engels. (The others were the monarchy and the
republic.) Among the most important conclusions of Marx's studies of
France was that the dominant economic class in a society may not necessarily be the class that has political control of the state. The second coup
of Bonaparte removed the representatives of the bourgeoisie from control of the state apparatus. The state then became relatively independent
of the contending classes. However, this independence did not mean that
it was neutral in the class struggle. Bonaparte operated it consciously to
safeguard the bourgeois order and in many instances was able to perform
actions to advance capitalist interests which the bourgeois representatives had been unable to do when in state control.
   The uncovering of the period when the state assumed a relatively
independent position led Engels to reformulate the relationship between
the class struggle and the state. The state is, ''as a rule, the state of the
most powerful, economically dominant class, which, through the medium
of the state, becomes also the politically dominant class, and thus
acquires new means of holding down and exploiting the oppressed
class.'' This can be seen as both the normal case and the tendency of
development. But there are exceptions. ''Periods occur in which the

warring classes balance each other so nearly that the state power, as ostensible mediator acquires, for the moment, a certain degree of independence of both." In addition to the case of France, Engels mentioned also as examples "the absolute monarchy of the seventeenth and eighteenth centuries, which held the balance between the nobility and the class of burghers" and "the New German Empire of the Bismark nation [where] capitalists and workers are balanced against each other and equally cheated for the benefit of the impoverished Prussian cabbage Junkers" (*The Origin of the Family, Private Property, and the State*, p. 168).

Bourgeois Consciousness: Functional consciousness of the capitalist class. The consciousness of the bourgeoisie is not restricted to the minority who actually occupy bourgeois class positions. If capitalists are possessive about their material power, they are not as stingy with their consciousness; they prefer necessarily to have other classes to see things their way. Hence, Marx and Engels wrote in *The German Ideology* (p. 67) that "the ideas of the ruling class are in every epoch the ruling ideas, i.e., the class which is the ruling *material* force of society, is at the same time its ruling *intellectual* force. . . . The ruling ideas are nothing more than the ideal expression of the dominant material relationships." The "ideal expression of the dominant material relationships" is disseminated to other classes in content and often through the form of the schools, press, work place, market, family, and other institutions. The capitalist mode of consciousness, as an aspect of the mode of production, is a functional necessity that must be produced and reproduced intergenerationally. It has to reflect the principles of commodity production, class exploitation, and alienation. Bourgeois consciousness includes assumptions that human beings are inherently unequal in worth (therefore the hierarchy of classes is necessary to match the supposed hierarchy of natural ability); the vast majority of people are inherently lazy and can only be motivated by material rewards and discipline (the carrot and the stick); individualism, competitiveness, and selfishness represent truly human virtues ("each man is the other man's wolf"); and a society can only function if human beings are treated and organized as if they were commodities.

Bourgeoisie. *See* CAPITALIST CLASS.

Bourgeois Right: Concept developed by Marx in his "Critique of the Gotha Program" to characterize a transitional feature of socialist societies. Because there is an inequality of skills, strength, ability to work hard, and so forth, individuals will contribute more or less to the social product and hence draw out more or less accordingly. Distribution will be according to the productivity of the labor contributed. Bourgeois right thus means the application of equal standards which do not compensate for unequal abilities to labor. Those who have greater skills receive more and thus are in a higher class position. A person with six dependents receives the same as a single person for the same work even though the result of the application of equal standards results in substantive inequality. Marx probably called this bourgeois because it has parallels in many other spheres of bourgeois society. The point is well exemplified by Anatole France's famous comment that "the law in its magnificent equality forbids both the rich man and the poor man from sleeping under a bridge."

Bourgeois Socialism. *See* SOCIALISM, BOURGEOIS .

Branch of Production. *See* SPHERE AND BRANCH OF PRODUCTION.

Bureaucracy: From *bureau* (French for "desk"), bureaucracy literally means "government by the desks." The concept in Marx's and Engel's writings meant the structure of specialized functionaries in a governmental apparatus as distinct from the actual rulers or parliament. Since then the concept of bureaucracy has been expanded to include not only governmental functionaries but also the structure of specialized functionaries in private corporations who do the paperwork as distinct from the actual production work.

C

Capital: In popular usage, the accumulated assets of a person, family, or business as opposed to income for a specific period. The origin of the word *capital* is derived from the word for cattle; cattle were one of the first forms of wealth. The Marxian concept, however, differs. It defines capital not as wealth that has already created but rather as wealth that is in the process of being created. Capital is a "self-expanding value." Capital is the form of exchange value that is or potentially will be invested in either the production of surplus value or the appropriation of surplus value which was produced elsewhere. Marx analyzed three investment possibilities for the realization of surplus value which correspond to the three fundamental types of capital in a capitalist society: merchant capital, moneylenders' capital, and productive capital. In its basis though, "Capital is *stored-up labor*" (Marx, *Economic and Philosophic Manuscripts of 1844*, p. 38).

See also ACCUMULATION OF CAPITAL; CENTRALIZATION OF CAPITAL; CIRCULATION OF CAPITAL; COMMERCIAL CAPITAL; CONCENTRATION OF CAPITAL; CONSTANT AND VARIABLE CAPITAL; CREDIT CAPITAL; ESTATE CAPITAL; FICTITIOUS CAPITAL; FIXED AND CIRCULATING CAPITAL; MONEY AND REAL CAPITAL; MONEY, COMMODITY, INDUSTRIAL, AND PRODUCTIVE CAPITAL; MONEY-DEALING CAPITAL; MONEYLENDERS' CAPITAL; NATURAL AND MOVABLE CAPITAL; INDIVIDUAL AND SOCIAL CAPITAL; INTEREST-BEARING CAPITAL; LAND CAPITAL; PRIMITIVE ACCUMULATION OF CAPITAL; STATE CAPITAL; USURERS' CAPITAL; VALUE, TECHNICAL, AND ORGANIC COMPOSITIONS OF CAPITAL; GENERAL LAW OF CAPITALIST ACCUMULATION.

Capitalism: Mode of production characterized by the private ownership of the means of production. The major form of exploitation and production of wealth is based on the labor of the working class. Capitalism requires that the means of production be commodities which can be traded among the capitalist class and that labor power be a commodity which the working class sells.

See also GOAL OF CAPITALISM; FUNDAMENTAL CONTRADICTION OF CAPITALISM.

Capitalist Class: Dominant class of capitalist societies whose position is based on their ownership and control of income-producing property (e.g., factories, large commercial establishments, and financial institutions) where workers are employed. By capitalist is meant "the owners of the means of social production and employers of wage-labor" (Engels, "The Communist Manifesto," p. 108n). Marx and Engels used the terms *bourgeoisie* and *upper middle class* as synonyms for the capitalist class.

Cartel: Working agreement among companies in a particular field to regulate their production or prices cooperatively in order to maximize profits. Engels wrote:

> In every country this is taking place through the big industrialists of a certain branch joining a cartel for the regulation of production. A committee fixes the quantity to be produced by each establishment and is the final authority for distributing the incoming orders. Occasionally even international cartels were established, as between the English and German iron industries. [Comment to Marx's text in Vol. 3 of *Capital*, p. 438]

Category: Term used by Marx for the empirical concepts of economics, or those concepts which sought to portray economic processes. For example, slavery is a category representing the institution of slavery. Categories as such are historically specific concepts, that is, concepts that are valid only for particular historical periods. "He [Proudon] has not perceived that *economic categories* are only *abstract expressions* of these actual relations and only remain true while these relations exist . . . the political-economic categories [are] abstract expressions of the real, transitory, historical social relations" (*Letters*, Marx to P. V. Annenkov, December 28, 1846). There is a second sense in which the concept of category is used. Engels wrote, "Two philosophical tendencies, the metaphysical with fixed categories, the dialectical (Aristotle and especially Hegel) with fluid categories. . . ." (*Dialectics of Nature*, p. 271). That dialectical categories are "fluid" does not mean that their meanings are imprecise or vague; rather it means that a category as an intellectual construct of a real process presupposes that processes interpenetrate and hence that what the category reflects is not rigidly separated (pidgeonholed) from what other categories treat.

Centralization of Capital: Marxian economic term for the amassing of capital in one place by the combination of the individual capitals of two or more capitalists. Competitive pressures are the usual cause of the centralization of capital: one capitalist takes over the capital of a bankrupt competitor or several capitalists combine their capitals to gain the competitive market advantage of size. The merger movement is the synonym in contemporary corporate literature for the centralization of capital. The centralization of capital results from changes in the distribution of already existing capitals.

Chartism: British working class movement of the 1830s and 1840s. The chartists drew up several petitions requesting such rights as universal suffrage, the secret ballot, shorter work hours, and higher wages. When these were rejected by Parliament, they resorted to a general strike which was put down by troops. After 1848 the Chartist movement died down, but its ideas continued to be influential.

Chiliasm: Medieval peasant movement based on the mystical belief that Christ would return to earth and create a thousand-year society of justice, equality, and well-being. The name *Chiliasm* comes from the Greek work *chilias*, which means "thousand."

Christian Socialism. *See* SOCIALISM, CHRISTIAN.

Circulating Capital. *See* FIXED AND CIRCULATING CAPITAL.

Circulation of Capital: The cycle in any capitalist business of investing capital in order to make a profit and then reinvesting part of the return to start the process over again. Marx wrote:

> The circular movement of capital takes place in three stages. . . . First stage: The capitalist appears as a buyer on the commodity- and the labor-market; his money is transformed into commodities, or it goes through the circulation act M—C. Second stage: Productive consumption of the purchased commodities by the capitalist. He acts as a capitalist producer of commodities; his capital passes through the process of production. The result is a commodity of more value than that of the elements entering into its production. Third stage: The capitalist returns to the market as a seller; his commodities are turned into money, or they pass through the circulation act C—M. [*Capital*, vol. 2, p. 25]

Circulation of Commodities: The exchange in whatever form of one product for another, which can take the form of simple trading, barter, or buying or selling.

Civilization: Term used by Lewis H. Morgan, the nineteenth-century American anthropologist whose studies influenced Engel's theory of the development of the family. Civilization is the third period after the descent of humans from the animal kingdom—the first two were savagery and barbarism. Civilization is "the period in which knowledge of the further working up of natural products, of industry proper, and of art was acquired" (Engels, *The Origin of the Family, Private Property, and the State*, p. 29).

Civil Society: Term used by Marx and Engels in two different ways. In the first, civil society meant the material economic structure, as opposed to political forms or ideological life, of any society. Marx and Engels wrote, "civil society embraces the whole material intercourse of individuals within a definite stage of the development of productive forces. It embraces the whole commercial and industrial life of a given stage, and, insofar, transcends the state and the nation, though on the other hand again, it must assert itself in its external relations as nationality and internally must organize itself as state . . . the social organization evolving directly out of production and intercourse, which in all ages forms the basis of the state and of the rest of the idealistic superstructure" (*The German Ideology*, p. 98). In the second use of the term, civil society meant the specific type of material intercourse of capitalist societies and as such was identical to bourgeois society.

Class: From the verb "classify," refers to categories used for placing people when there are qualitative socioeconomic differences between them. The category of class is based fundamentally upon economic function. This fundamental aspect of class is called the class *in itself*. It represents the dialectical interrelationship between the structuring of economies and the differential structuring of the lives of different categories of people; it flows from the Marxist analysis of political economies. But the Marxist concept of class includes more. It includes how people perceive their position (class consciousness) and how they act upon that perception (class organization). Class consciousness and class organization are aspects of the class *for itself* or the dialectical interrelationship between categories of people and the making of history. The dialectical quality of the Marxist concept of class is clear. Class formation from *in itself* to *for itself* is a tendency, not a static fact or given. The concept of class captures not only the statistical distribution of a people but also the developing subjective and organizational forces of a people. Classes are both made by, and makers of, history. The concept of class encompasses passive and active elements, determined and determining qualities, objectivity and subjectivity.

The separate individuals form a class only insofar as they have to carry on a common battle against another class; in other respects they are on hostile terms with each other as competitors. On the other hand, the class in its turn assumes an independent existence as against the individuals, so that the latter find their conditions of life predetermined, and have their position in life and hence their personal development assigned to them by their class, thus becoming subsumed under it. [Ibid., p. 85]

Class was also used loosely by Marx and Engels to indicate subclasses of an overall class, e.g., the class of bankers.

See also CAPITALIST CLASS; LANDLORD CLASS; MIDDLE CLASS; NOBILITY; ARISTOCRACY; PEASANTS; RULING CLASS; SLAVES; TRANSITION CLASS; WORKING CLASS; COMMERCIAL BOURGEOISIE; INDUSTRIAL BOURGEOISIE; PETTY BOURGEOISIE; CLASS STRUGGLE.

Class Consciousness: The ideas that reflect the material existence of particular classes. As class members become aware of their common identity, interests, and political goals, class consciousness develops. It is an attribute of a community, of communal action, the "we" identification. It is the intersubjective factor which mediates societal oppression and successful revolution against that oppression. Class consciousness represents both a process of development and a goal-oriented given. That is, the overall content of class consciousness is a given that corresponds to the historical interests of the class in question. As such, it does not mean the particular attitudes of class members at any particular time. This empirical consciousness of the class, which is at best approximately measured by such devices as public opinion polls, has no necessary correlation with the historical content of class consciousness as such. There is a distinction between the empirical consciousness of class members at any particular time and their latent historical class consciousness. Often the latent historical class consciousness manifests itself in periods of revolutionary crisis or intense class struggle when individual class members interpret reality through the mediation of the class as a frame of reference and its collective as opposed to individual interests. There is a trajectory of class consciousness which differs with each class. The contents of their developing class consciousnesses will differ accordingly.

See also BOURGEOIS CONSCIOUSNESS; PEASANT CONSCIOUSNESS; PETTY BOURGEOIS CONSCIOUSNESS; FALSE CONSCIOUSNESS; and WORKING CLASS CONSCIOUSNESS.

Class Contradiction. *See* CONTRADICTION.

Class for Itself. *See* CLASS.

Class in Itself. *See* CLASS.

Class Struggle: The actualization of the potential for strife which exists in any society based on classes that have objectively antagonistic interests. Marx and Engels began "The Communist Manifesto" (p. 108) with the proposition that "the history of all hitherto existing society is the history of class struggles." Class struggles exist manifestly and latently, consciously and unconsciously, in clear and subtle forms in all class societies. They run the range from psychological and personality conflicts between classes to union organizing to open rebellion and revolution.

Clerical Socialism. *See* SOCIALISM, CHRISTIAN.

Colonial Market. *See* MARKET.

Colony: Territory whose government is directly administered by another country.

Commerce: The trading or marketing of goods and services.

Commercial Bourgeoisie: That sector of the bourgeoisie specializing in the circulation of commodities and money as opposed to actual production.
See also CAPITALIST CLASS.

Commercial Capital: Capital invested by the merchant to transform produced commodities into money, i.e., to sell produced commodities. Commercial capital and money-dealing capital are the two forms of merchant's capital. (See Marx, *Capital*, vol. 3, chapter 16.)

Commodity: Product of labor which is produced in order to be exchanged in a market transaction. All commodities are products of labor, but not all products of labor are commodities. For example, if a loaf of bread is consumed by the baker, it is not a commodity; it only becomes a commodity when it is intended to be sold or traded to another. The commodity is the economic "cell" or unit of analysis of capitalist society.
See also CIRCULATION OF COMMODITIES.

Commodity Capital: *See* MONEY; COMMODITY; INDUSTRIAL CAPITAL; PRODUCTIVE CAPITAL.

Commodity Market: Inclusive term for all the arenas in which products of labor are bought, sold, or generally exchanged.

Commodity Production: The making of goods intended to be exchanged in a market transaction as opposed to the making of goods intended for direct consumption by the maker.

Communism: Two related meanings. First, communism is the mode of production that will succeed the capitalist mode of production. It is characterized by common ownership of the means of production, the absence of class divisions, distribution according to need, the absence of a repressive state apparatus, and social planning. Second, communism means the set of beliefs of those who advocate the overthrow of capitalist society as a means toward the goal of developing a Communist mode of production.

Concentration of Capital: Marxian economic term for the buildup through production of large quantities of capital in particular locations.

Concept: Intellectual construct that summarizes the general properties of an object of thought and analysis. What distinguishes the Marxian meaning of *concept* is its role as a dialectical tool of analysis. In summing the general properties, the Marxian concept separates inessential, or accidental, from essential properties in order to penetrate appearances and uncover essences of reality. The process of abstraction implied by concept construction is thus meant to be a movement toward, not away from, reality. In Hegelian writing, ''notion'' is sometimes used as a synonym for concept.
See also ABSTRACTION; APPEARANCE AND ESSENCE.

Concrete and Abstract Labor: Labor on one level of analysis is conceived in terms of what it actually (concretely) does, that is for example, build a house or repair a road. On another level labor is conceived in terms of how it is related to the accumulation of capital, regardless of what its concrete form is. The latter is a conception of abstract labor; in other words, it is *abstracted* from its empirical, concrete form to its function in the essential economic accumulation of capital. Labor as the creator of use values is concrete, qualitative, particular labor; as the creator of exchange values, it is abstract and quantitative.

Congealed Labor. *See* LIVING AND DEAD LABOR.

Consanguine Family: Form of group marriage which predated the modern nuclear family. According to Lewis H. Morgan, the American anthropologist on whose research Engels relied, the consanguine family was the first stage of the family, which followed the original condition of promiscuous sexual intercourse. In the consanguine family several generations live in the same household. Those of the same generation, including brothers and sisters, are in a group marriage; hence, limited incest prevails. However, ancestors and descendants are not in the same marriage group, and hence, among them sexual relations were forbidden. Engels described the consanguine family as follows:

> Here the marriage groups are ranged according to generations: all the grandfathers and grandmothers within the limits of the family are all mutual husbands and wives, the same being the case with their children, the fathers and mothers, whose children will again form a third circle of common mates, their children—the great-grandchildren of the first—in turn, forming a fourth circle. Thus, in this form of the family, only ancestors and descendants, parents and children, are excluded from the rights and obligations (as we would say) of marriage with one another. Brothers and sisters, male and female cousins of the first, second and more remote degrees are all mutually brothers and sisters and precisely because of this are all mutually husbands and wives. At this stage the relation of brother and sister includes the exercise of sexual intercourse with one another as a matter of course. In its typical form, such a family would consist of the descendants of a pair, among whom, again, the descendants of each degree are all brothers and sisters, and, precisely for that reason, all mutual husbands and wives. [*The Origin of the Family, Private Property and the State*, p. 37]

See PROMISCUOUS SEXUAL INTERCOURSE.

Consciousness: Mental awareness of experience. Awareness, or consciousness, may be a valid or invalid mental reflection of experience and material reality. At its base, Marx and Engels wrote, "consciousness can never be anything else than conscious being, and the being of men is their actual life-process" (*The German Ideology*, p. 42). In the case of an invalid mental reflection, Engels spoke of "false consciousness."
See also BEING; CLASS CONSCIOUSNESS; FALSE CONSCIOUSNESS; IDEOLOGY; SUBJECT.

Constant and Variable Capital: Marxian economic categories to distinguish the different functions of the means of production and labor power in the creation of surplus value. In a production process the means of production are constant capital because they function as intermediaries which preserve and transfer value that was originally created by labor in its journey from raw material to finished product. Labor power is variable capital because it is the element in the production process that accounts for the creation of surplus value at each step. The capitalist can *vary* labor time, the pace of work, and thus surplus value production of the workers. *"Constant capital* is that part of capital which consists of raw material and machinery. *Variable capital* that part which is exchanged for labor" (*Letters*, Marx to Engels, July 6, 1863).

Consumption: The act of using up a good in order to satisfy a need. "In consumption the product . . . becomes the direct object and servant of an individual need, which its use satisfies." (Marx, Introduction to *A Contribution to the Critique of Political Economy*). Production, distribution, consumption, and exchange are phases of an interrelated process with the mode of production being the decisive phase. (See *ibid.*)
See also PRODUCTIVE AND INDIVIDUAL CONSUMPTION.

Contradiction: Category used in dialectical logic to represent the premise that opposing forces in contention are the essential feature of all processes of development. The resolution of the struggle between the opposing forces generates a new synthesis, that is, further development.

> . . . as soon as we consider things in their motion, their change, their life, their reciprocal influence on one another. Then we immediately become involved in contradictions. Motion itself is a contradiction: even simple mechanical change of position can only come about through a body being at one and the same moment of time both in one place and in another place, being in one and the same place and also not in it. And the continuous origination and simultaneous solution of this contradiction is precisely what motion is. . . . If simple mechanical change of place contains a contradiction, that is even more true of the higher forms of motion of matter, and especially of organic life and its development. We saw above that life consists precisely and primarily in this—that a being is at each moment itself and yet something else. Life is therefore also a contradiction which is present in things and processes themselves, and which constantly originates and resolves itself; and as soon as the contradiction ceases, life, too, comes to an end, and death steps in. We likewise saw that also in the sphere of thought we could not escape contradictions. . . . [Engels, *Anti-Duhring*, p. 144]

There are several different types of contradictions. First is a distinction that is implicit in Marx's work but made explicit by Mao and others is between nonantagonistic and antagonistic contradictions. A nonantagonistic contradiction, in general, is a contradiction which is an inherent feature of all forms of development such as the contradiction between motion and rest. Applied to history, nonantagonistic contradictions are all types of contradictions that are common to all processes of development and not a particular feature of modes of production based on class and property divisions. Mao and others sometimes used the term nonantagonistic contradiction in another sense to refer to "contradictions among the people," that is, those contradictions based on personal rather than antagonistic class differences. Though contradictions are a general feature of all reality; antagonistic contradictions are particular types of contradictions generated by the contexts of modes of production based on property and class divisions. An antagonistic contradiction thus has its origin in pre-Communist modes of production and would not exist in the Communist mode of production. Class and economic contradictions are the two most general antagonistic contradictions.

A set of distinctions on a different basis is between historical, economic, and class contradictions. A historical contradiction is nonantagonistic and occurs in all modes of production. It is the contention between "what is" and "what is in the process of becoming" in historical development. The historical contradiction results in both quantitative and qualitative change and is related to the paradoxical premise of dialectics that change is the only constant feature of reality.

An economic contradiction is a contradiction located in the economic structure of society. The overall economic contradictions of pre-Communist societies exist when either the internal economic processes of development of a society operate at cross purposes or where the conditions for production fetter the growth of production. The result of an economic contradiction when carried to sufficient exacerbation is an economic crisis such as a depression or recession. Marx and Engels identified two overall economic contradictions. The first, the contradiction between the forces and relations of production, exists in all pre-Communist societies. The potential growth of the forces of production is fettered by the context (the relations of production) in which they develop. The second, the increasingly socialized character of production and the capitalistic appropriation, is specific to capitalist societies. Production is increasingly interdependent; yet, each capitalist plans for her or his own profit maximization. Hence while production is increasingly socialized, and the relations among the decision-makers are anarchic.

Cooperative Labor: The process where "numerous laborers work together side by side, whether in one and the same process, or in different but connected processes'' (Marx, *Capital*, p. 308). Cooperative labor represents an important step forward in the social organization of the labor process. It has a number of advantages over isolated individual labor. For example, large numbers of workers can lift heavier weights than workers can singly; large numbers of workers can be concentrated to bring in a harvest when delays in time can be costly. If a large number of workers is concentrated in one place, they can share tools and the structure within which they work.

Corn Laws: Laws first established in England in the 1400s that placed a high tariff on imported corn to protect the domestic growers' market. In the first half of the nineteenth century the existence of the corn laws became an issue because the industrial capitalists favored their repeal so that the price would go down and correspondingly the cost of living of the working class. The latter change would mean that the capitalists could lower wages. The landed aristocracy opposed the repeal as being against their economic interests. The corn laws were finally repealed in 1846. The controversy over the corn laws demonstrated two things about class development. First, the corn laws controversy was a manifestation of the conflict between town and country in terms of the economic interest of their respective ruling classes. Second, the repeal of the corn laws showed that the capitalists had gained the upper hand over the landed aristocracy in the governance of the English state.

Corvée: System of labor exploitation in feudalism where peasants were granted use of land in return for working the lands of the nobility for a set number of days each week.

Cost of Production: The amount of capital invested in labor power and means of production in a particular production process.

Cost-price: The amount of capital invested in the production of a commodity. The exchange value of a commodity less the surplus value produced equals the cost-price. Cost-price is a synonym for cost of production.

> The part of capital consumed in the production of a commodity (the capital, constant and variable, advanced for its production *minus* the utilized but not actually consumed portion of the *fixed* capital) appears now as the *cost price* of the commodity; for to the capitalist that part of the value of the commodity which *he* has to pay for is *its* cost price, while the unpaid labor it contains is not included in *its* price, from his point of view. [Letters, Marx to Engels, April 30, 1868]

Counterrevolution: The overthrow of a revolutionary government by the former ruling class. Frequently after a revolution the former rulers will reorganize and attempt to recapture state power. The danger of counter-revolution was one of the reasons that motivated Marx to develop his concept of the dictatorship of the proletariat.
See also DICTATORSHIP OF THE PROLETARIAT; REVOLUTION.

Coup d'état: French term used to describe an overthrow of state power without the participation of the masses. The most common case of a *coup d' état* is that executed by a group of military officers who seize control of the top of state power.

Craft: Originally meant a manual work skill which required extensive training, apprenticeship, and certification in order to be practiced.

Creative Labor: Human labor which combines mental planning with manual execution. Creative labor is a defining characteristic of the essence of human nature which is largely suppressed under conditions of capitalist alienation. Marx wrote in *Capital* (p. 174) that

> A spider conducts operations that resemble those of a weaver, and a bee puts to shame many an architect in the construction of her cells. But what distinguishes the worst architect from the best of bees is this, that the architect raises his structure in imagination before he erects it in reality. At the end of every labor-process, we get a result that already existed in the imagination of the laborer at its commencement.

Credit: The value which is advanced in a business transaction when a commodity is sold, not for money, but rather for a promissory note or pledge to pay the money and usually a quantity of interest at a specified time in the future.
See also BANK NOTE; BILL OF EXCHANGE; FICTITIOUS CAPITAL; DISCOUNTING; NATIONAL DEBT.

Credit Capital: Capital which is borrowed from another.

Crisis Theory: The body of Marxist writing which analyzes the causes, timing, nature, and consequences of economic depressions and recessions in capitalist societies. The origin of crisis theory is Marx's contention that periodic economic crises are one of the structural contradictions of the capitalist mode of production. For example, one analyzed by Marx is the crisis of overproduction. Due to the lack of centralized economic planning, more products are produced than there is an effective demand for. Consequently workers **are laid off until** the surplus products are sold. But since the workers **as consumers** now have less income, the effective demand decreases even more. **The** result is a recession and, in more serious cases, depression.

Critique: An examination or analysis that probes for what is incorrect and what is correct in an object of study. A critique is not synonymous with a simple attack or criticism.

D

Dead Labor. *See* LIVING AND DEAD LABOR.

Definition: Intellectual construct which describes the essential properties of an object of thought. A good definition is the result of an investigation which has both penetrated appearances and separated accidental properties in order to uncover the essence of an object. Engels warned against reifying definitions, since essences are always in the process of change.

> To science definitions are worthless because always inadequate. The only real definition is the development of the thing itself, but this is no longer a definition. . . . On the other hand, *for ordinary purposes*, a brief exposition of the commonest and at the same time most significant features of a so-called definition is often useful and even necessary, and can do no harm if no more is expected of it than it can convey. [Engels, *Anti-Duhring*, p. 405]

See also ABSTRACTION; CONCEPT; ESSENCE AND APPEARANCE.

Deism: Seventeenth- and eighteenth-century philosophical and religious movement which saw God as the primary cause of the existence of reality, but not as intervening in the development of that reality. Deism specifically repudiated belief in miracles and divine intervention in favor of seeking knowledge through the discovery of the laws of nature. Deism represented a thought current that in some ways contributed to the early development of a materialist as opposed to religious outlook. Deism developed in England (Lord Herbert and Lord Shaftesbury in the seventeenth century), France (Voltaire, eighteenth century), and in North America.

Determination: Category in dialectical logic for expressing the manner in which causality occurs. A factor or complex of factors "determines"—in the sense of conditions as opposed to mechanistically causing—the existence or a change in the existence of another factor or complex of factors.

Dialectics: The logical system underlying Marxian science. Originally dialectics, from the Greek *dialego* (to discuss or debate), was a method developed by Socrates and others to attain truth by discussing and examining questions from different points of view. They assumed that any one point of view was necessarily one-sided. The Socratic concept of dialectics, however, is not the same as the Marxian. In the Marxian meaning, dialectics is the system of logic in science that follows the logic of development of history and nature. The distinguishing feature of dialectical logic is that it is premised on the understanding that reality is a totality characterized by change, interrelationships, and contradictions. The most significant characteristic of aspects of human and natural reality is their development and interrelationships. An aspect of human reality cannot be validly examined unto itself without relating it to its process of change and its environment. Thus Engels described dialectics as "the science of universal inter-connection" and "of the most general laws of *all* motion" (*Dialectics of Nature*, pp. 27 and 353). Marx's dialectic developed in a significant respect from his critique of G. W. F. Hegel's idealist dialectic.

See also DIALECTICAL IDEALISM; DIALECTICAL MATERIALISM; HISTORICAL MATERIALISM; CATEGORY; CONTRADICTION; DETERMINATION; ESSENCE AND APPEARANCE; FORCES; IN ITSELF AND FOR ITSELF; LAWS OF DIALECTICS; MANIFESTATION; MOMENT; MOTION AND FORCE; NATURE AND HISTORY DIALECTIC; NODAL POINT; NOTION; NEGATION; SPIRAL FORM OF DEVELOPMENT; SUBLATE; THESIS-ANTITHESIS-SYNTHESIS; TOTALITY; RELATION; IMMANENT; INDIVIDUAL, PARTICULAR, UNIVERSAL; MEDIATION.

Dialectical Idealism: Term for philosophies which employ a dialectical logic to elaborate the premise that ideas are logically prior to material things in reality. The Hegelian system is the primary example. For a description of dialectical idealism, see Engels, "Socialism: Scientific and Utopian."
See also DIALECTICS; IDEALISM.

Dialectical Materialism: Post-Marx term applied to the philosophy developed by Marx and Engels. Dialectical materialism applies a dialectical logic to elaborate the premises that in history objective human activity and being are logically prior to ideas while in nature material things are prior.

Dictatorship of the Proletariat: One of the forms a state can assume during socialism. Marx wrote in "The Critique of the Gotha Program" (p. 26) that "between capitalist and communist society lies the period of

the revolutionary transformation of the one into the other. Corresponding to this is also a political transition period in which the state can be
nothing but the revolutionary dictatorship of the proletariat.'' The
socialist period between capitalism and communism is thus both a period
in which revolutionary transformation has to be purposively pushed
forward and the state has to be a powerful force. The dictatorship of the
proletariat simply means that the state power is wielded in the interests of
the working classes, and the former oppressing classes are stripped of
their power to govern society by means such as through the ownership of
newspapers or factories. The workers' state thus, aside from protecting
the revolutionary process from internal counterrevolutionaries and
external enemies, has the function of being an organ used for transforming the society. ''What I [Marx] did that was new was to prove:
(1) that the *existence of classes* is only bound up with *particular historical
phases in the development of production*, (2) that the class struggle
necessarily leads to the *dictatorship of the proletariat*, (3) that this
dictatorship itself only constitutes the transition to the *abolition of all
classes* and to a *classless society''* (*Letters*, Marx to J. Weydemeyer,
March 5, 1852). Dictatorship today is usually taken to mean that a
person or small group governs without the consent of the ruled. Marx's
meaning or use of the term was different, since it referred to rule not of a
person or small group but rather to that of a class or at least its legitimate
representative, such as a political party. Presumably in Marx's conception the dictatorship of the proletariat implies the consent of the majority, the proletariat, and only the nonconsent of the former ruling class,
the bourgeoisie.

Differential Ground Rent. *See* GROUND RENT.

Discounting: Financial term for the practice of a bank purchasing a
promissory note from a creditor at less than its full value. The bank
deducts interest for the amount of time still left on the note. For example, if A makes a loan to B for $10,000 at a rate of interest of 10 percent
for one year, B will have to pay A $11,000 at the end of one year. A may
need money before the end of the year. In such a case he or she would sell
the promissory note from B to a bank for, say, $10,400.

Distribution: Economic term for the share that each individual receives
of the total production of a society. Concretely, distribution is the different rates of income that individuals receive. Production, distribution,
consumption, and exchange are phases of an interrelated process with
the mode of production being the decisive phase. See Marx, Introduction

to *A Contribution to the Critique of Political Economy*.
See also MODE OF DISTRIBUTION.

Division of Labor: Sociological term for any specialization of tasks in production. Marx distinguished between the division of labor in society as a whole and that in the workshop. The division of labor in the former application is associated with two developments. First, the increase of the division of labor accompanies technological progress. That is, as society develops technologically, work in commerce, manufacturing, and other areas is done in more different places by more different people than is the case with work in agriculture. But second, in the capitalist context, the potential for progress is somewhat diminished because private property competition precludes full economic planning to coordinate the different parts of the societal division of labor. Division of labor within the work place means "the breaking down of the particular labor which produces a definite commodity into a series of simple and co-ordinated operations divided up amongst different workers" (Marx, *Theories of Surplus Value*, part 3, p. 268). Marx notes here that unlike the societal division of labor, the capitalist is able to employ the utmost of planning to increase relative surplus value production regardless of the alienating effects upon the workers. (See *Capital*, chapter 14, section 4.)

Doctrinaire. *See* DOGMATISM.

Dogmatism: Pejorative term for the practice of treating Marxism as a set of established truths rather than as a method for scientific understanding and changing the world. The term originates with the Catholic church where dogma were established tenets beyond questioning. *Doctrinaire* is a synonym for dogmatism.

Domestic Market. *See* MARKET.

Dualism: Philosophical term for the premise that reality is based ultimately on not one (as in monism) but two separate principles, e.g., spirit and matter.
See also MONISM.

E

Eclecticism: In Greek philosophy the term *Eclectics* was applied to those philosophers who neither adhered to any particular school of philosophy nor developed an independent view but rather chose elements from the different schools as it pleased their purposes, regardless of how inconsistent and out of context the particular elements might be with each other. In Marx's time and today the term means largely the same, although it is extended to apply to the development of social, economic, and political theories in the same manner.

Economic Contradiction. *See* CONTRADICTION.

Economic Determinism: The view that only strictly economic factors have causal importance in history. Marx and Engels are often accused of having been economic determinists, but they explicitly rejected that view. (See Engels, letter to J. Bloch, September 21, 1890.)

Economic Structure of Society: "The totality of the relations of production" (Marx, Preface to *A Contribution to the Critique of Political Economy*). The economic structure is thus the totality of all relations whose object is production. As such the structure is not narrowly defined to be a limited proportion of social life that has overwhelming importance, but rather it is identified much more broadly with the major proportion of social life. To the extent that any social relation is related to production in one form or another it is a part of the economic structure. Some social relations such as that between capital and labor can be easily categorized in that manner. But there are also other production relations such as those surrounding the family.
See also RELATIONS OF PRODUCTION.

Economic Surplus: The amount that the combined labor of a society produces in excess of its current level of consumption in any mode of production.

Economism: The overemphasis on strictly economic developments in explanation and consequent downplaying of other factors. The fallacy of economism has been critiqued in a number of areas. In trade-union socialist politics, economism is the belief that workers should only struggle for immediate economic goals, reserving political goals for political parties. The struggle for economic goals, the economists believe, will eventually result in socialist consciousness. In historical research and vulgar Marxism, economism takes the form of the belief that historical events are explainable by tracing only the narrow economic self-interests of the actors involved. In social science, economism is related to the belief that the laws of the natural and social worlds are interchangeable, that the social world develops in a Darwinian evolutionary fashion, which is determined by laws over which humans have no control. In socialist movements, economism is manifested in the belief that socialism will come about because of automatic evolutionary progress due to the development of economic tendencies. Marx, Engels, Lenin, Gramsci, and others have criticized economist assumptions by emphasizing the importance of ideological struggle and organization.

Elementary Factors of the Labor Process: The workers' activity, what they work on, and the instruments of their labor. Marx wrote that the elementary factors of the labor process were "1, the personal activity of man, i.e. work itself, 2, the subject of that work, and 3, its instruments" (*Capital*, p. 174).
See also INSTRUMENTS OF LABOR.

Elementary Form of Value. Category developed by Marx in *Capital*, Chapter 1, Section 3 for analyzing exchange value equations between commodities and the development from simple to complex forms of exchange. The elementary form of value expresses the exchange value of a commodity by how much of a different commodity to which it is equivalent; for example, one avocado is worth the same in exchange value as one mango. This form of value exchange first appears historically in primitive economic conditions where occasional barter is the only form of exchange as thus where exchange ratios have to be calculated anew for each different commodity.
See EXCHANGE VALUE; EXPANDED FORM OF VALUE; GENERAL FORM OF VALUE; MONEY; MONEY FORM OF VALUE; RELATIVE AND EQUIVALENT FORMS OF VALUE; UNIVERSAL EQUIVALENT.

Empiricism: The methodological premise that all knowledge is derived from direct experience; thus the task of science is to record the data of the world as directly experienced. Marxists view this premise as superficial, scientifically incorrect, and ideologically loaded in favor of the status quo because the way the world appears and the way it really is are often different. A reasoning process must penetrate beneath the level of surface appearances in order to uncover what structures or determines those appearances.

Enclosure Acts: A series of laws and legal measures in England which transformed use of the medieval common lands from use by all for grazing and firewood gathering to the exclusive property and prerogative of the landlord. The Enclosure Acts were one of the historical events which undermined the economic viability of the peasant household and thus had the effect of driving peasants from the land.

Endogamy: The practice of marrying only within the group or tribe.

Equivalent Form of Value. *See* RELATIVE AND EQUIVALENT FORMS OF VALUE.

Essence and Appearance: A distinction in dialectics between reality and the way that reality is experienced. The frequent disjuncture between the two generates the scientific need for different levels of analysis. If there were not a difference between essence and appearance, there would be no need for science because science penetrates the appearances of things to discover their essence. Essence is the core of any process or formation that determines, that is, influences how that process will manifest itself concretely. The appearance is the level of surface empirical reality which has been determined or influenced by its essence. The appearance is sometimes called the manifestation of the essence.

Estate: Sociological term for the various strata in feudalism. In medieval European feudalism the various social strata—nobility, church, townspeople—were assigned definite privileges, e.g. in governing, in accord with their position.

Estate is related to status or standing in the world. But whereas status is a subjective recognition of standing, with estates status distinctions were formalized into definite corresponding privileges. "Estates here in the historical sense of the estates of feudalism, estates with definite and limited privileges. The revolution of the bourgeoisie abolished the estates and their privileges. Bourgeoisie society knows only *classes*" (Note by Engels to Marx, *The Poverty of Philosophy*, p. 151).

Estate Capital: Type of capital owned by medieval guild masters. Their capital took the form of "a house, the tools of the craft, and the natural, hereditary customers . . . it descended from father to son. . . . Unlike modern capital, which can be assessed in money and which may be indifferently invested in this thing or that, this capital was directly connected with the particular work of the owner, inseparable from it and to this extent *estate* capital'' (Marx and Engels, *The German Ideology*, p. 74).

Exchange: Any activity which involves a transfer of a commodity or service. Production, distribution, consumption, and exchange are phases of an interrelated process with the mode of production being the decisive phase. (See Marx, Introduction to *A Contribution to the Critique of Political Economy*.)

Exchange Value: A quantitative measure of the relative value of commodities (products of labor) *vis-à-vis* one another which is determined by the relative amounts of social labor incorporated within each.
See also COMMODITY; LABOR THEORY OF VALUE.

Exogamy: The practice of allowing marriage outside the group or tribe.

Expanded Form of Value: Also called the Total Form of Value, a category developed by Marx in *Capital*, Chapter 1, Section 3 for analyzing exchange value equations between commodities and the development from simple to complex forms of exchange. The expanded form of value expresses the exchange value of a commodity by how much of numerous different commodities to which it is equivalent; for example, one avocado is worth the same in exchange value as one mango, or as one handkerchief, or as one pen, etc. This form of value exchange first appears historically when an economy has developed beyond occasional barter to the point where one particular commodity is continually exchanged for others and thus its value is known and established against the others.
See ELEMENTARY FORM OF VALUE; EXCHANGE VALUE; GENERAL FORM OF VALUE; MONEY; MONEY FORM OF VALUE; RELATIVE AND EQUIVALENT FORMS OF VALUE; UNIVERSAL EQUIVALENT.

Exploitation: The appropriation of the surplus labor of laboring classes by ruling classes in all class and property societies. In capitalist societies exploitation takes the form of the appropriation by the capitalists of the surplus value produced by the working class. The Marxian concept of exploitation is hence more specific than the popular concept, which considers exploitation to be the practice of using someone for your own purposes.

Expropriation: Term used by Marx and Engels in a variety of contexts to refer to removing control of the means of production from a particular individual, family, group, class, and so on. For example, when peasants are driven off the land, their land has been expropriated, or when small business owners lose their businesses because of competition from big businesses, they have been expropriated.

Extractive Industries: Industries whose aim is obtaining the products of nature. Marx defined extractive industries as "industries in which the material for labor is provided immediately by Nature, such as mining, hunting, fishing, and agriculture (so far as the latter is confined to breaking up virgin soil)" (*Capital*, p. 177).

F

Factionalism: Political term used to describe the practice of creating unnecessary divisions among members of an organization. Such divisions hinder and can destroy the unity necessary for the organization to be effective.

Falling Rate of Profit: Tendency predicted by Marx for capitalist societies. As constant capital replaces variable capital, i.e., as machines replace living labor in the production process with technological progress, there is less living labor to exploit for surplus value. Each unit produced hence contains a lower rate of profit for the capitalist. Marx predicted this as a tendency of development but also allowed for the development of offsetting tendencies which could mitigate its effects.

False Consciousness: Process of thought detached from material reality or based on an invalid reflection of material reality. The distorted form thought "is a process accomplished by the so-called thinker consciously, it is true, but with a false consciousness. The real forces impelling him remain unknown to him . . . hence he imagines false or seeming motive forces" (Engels, Letter to F. Mehring, July 14, 1893).
See CONSCIOUSNESS.

Family: In contemporary use, those related by common descent or through adoption. But, Engels noted that the meaning of the term has shifted from its earlier meanings.

> The word *familia* did not originally signify the ideal of our modern philistine, which is a compound of sentimentality and domestic discord. Among the Romans, in the beginning, it did not even refer to the married couple and their children, but to the slaves alone. *Famulus* means a household slave and *familia* signifies the totality of slaves belonging to one individual. Even in the time of Gaius the *familia, id est patrimonium* (that is, the inheritance) was bequeathed by will. The expression was invented by the Romans to describe a new social organism, the head of which had under him wife and children and a number of slaves, under Roman paternal power, with power of life and death over them all. . . . [Engels, *The Origin of the Family, Private Property and the State*, p. 58]

Given this history of the concept of the family, Marx wrote, "The modern family contains in embryo not only slavery (*servitus*) but serfdom also, since from the very beginning it is connected with agricultural services. It contains within itself in *miniature* all the antagonisms which later develop on a wide scale within society and its state" (quoted by Engels in *ibid*).

See also CONSANGUINE FAMILY; ENDOGAMY; EXOGAMY; GROUP MARRIAGE; HETAERISM; MONOGAMY; MOTHER RIGHT; PAIRING FAMILY; PATRIARCHAL FAMILY; POLYANDRY; POLYGAMY; PHRATRY; GENS; PROMISCUOUS SEXUAL INTERCOURSE; GENS, PHRATRY, TRIBE, NATION; PUNALUAN FAMILY; ZADRUGA.

Fetishism: In general the process whereby the products of humans appear to assume an independent existence and most likely return to oppress knowingly or unknowingly their creators. Religion was the first form of fetishism that Marx critiqued. He concluded that basically religious entities such as gods, though created by humans, assumed in their eyes an independent form. They appeared to be the creations of otherworldly forces. The most important secular source of human self-alienation, or fetishism, occurs because of the structure of commodity production. Commodities, though created by humans, assume in their eyes an independent, disconnected, and often oppressive form. The relationship between labor and the products of labor is turned upside down.

Feudal Socialism: *See* SOCIALISM, FEUDAL.

Feudalism: Mode of production based on agriculture, which immediately predates capitalism. Its best-known example was medieval Europe from the fall of the Roman Empire until the establishment of capitalism about the sixteenth century. Medieval European feudalism represents only one of many examples of feudalism which have occurred all over the world. Contemporary examples of feudal vestiges exist. The predominant characteristic of feudalism was decentralization. The central state power was weak; decentralized organs exercised the power. The economy was decentralized; there was no overall, centralized market. What accounted for social cohesion in a feudal society was neither blood ties (as in tribes) nor ties induced by economic dictates (as in capitalism). Rather social cohesion and order resulted from an elaborate system of personal relations. A powerful man gave protection to a weaker in return for military or economic services. A contract of sorts was made between the two, for life in most cases. The contract may involve the granting of the use of land to the weaker. These personal relations, of course, had an economic content. The major exploited class of a feudal society was the peasantry. They were the producers, and from their produce the nonproductive classes gained their livelihood.

See also APPRENTICE; CORVÉE; FIEF; GUILD; JOURNEYMAN; MASTER; QUIT RENT; SERFS AND FREE PEASANTS; USUFRUCT.

Fictitious Capital: Speculative form of capital created out of the credit system but backed by neither the actual money supply nor a bona fide business transaction. It occurs in times of low interest rates on money when bills of exchange begin to be directly exchanged as if they were money; they then perform the functions of a new supply of capital, albeit a fictitious capital, since it is not backed by anything. This is one of the bases of speculation and eventually a speculation crisis. The Soviet writer S. Menshikov defines fictitious capital as "capital invested securities (stocks or bonds) as distinct from 'real capital' which is invested in material wealth: structures, equipment, raw materials, etc., or used for employment of labor. The movement of fictitious capital, which has no intrinsic value is eventually determined by the movement of real capital, and reflects it. At the same time fictitious capital leads a life of its own and strongly affects real capital and the capitalist economy as a whole." (Menshikov, *Millionaires and Managers*, p. 12). All forms of promissory notes that are not backed up by a tangibly existing capital are also fictitious capital. In other words the owner of the promissory note could not take over a particular piece of property in lieu of payment. For example, government bonds are a form of fictitious capital. They represent the national debt and the owner of the bond has a claim on the *future* revenue of the state (its taxes), but his bond corresponds to no present existing capital. Fictitious capital represents an outgrowth of the credit system. Fictitious capital is interest-bearing capital: stocks and bonds that are bought and sold and thus have a circulation of their own on the market even though they do not represent actually existing capitals to which they could be converted. All government bonds are fictitious capital, since they represent already spent capital; stocks are fictitious capital to the extent that their value on the stock market is above and moves independently of the actual value of the capital that they represent as in the case of speculation. "All this paper actually represents nothing more than accumulated claims, or legal titles, to future production whose money or capital value represents either no capital at all, as in the case of state debts, or is regulated independently of the value of real capital which it represents" (Marx, *Capital*, vol. 3, p. 468).

Fief: Form of feudal property granted by a lord to a person of lesser status in return for a military, work, or other type of obligation.

Financial Aristocracy: Term used by Marx to indicate pure money capitalists who solely performed the function in a capitalist economy of investing money capital in ventures as opposed to actually planning and executing production. The development of capitalism "reproduces a new financial aristocracy, a new variety of parasites in the shape of promoters, speculators and simply nominal directors; a whole system of swindling and cheating by means of corporation promotion, stock issuance, and stock speculation" (Marx, *Capital*, vol. 3, p. 438). The financial aristocracy is an artifact of the growth of a credit system in capitalist economies. The aristocracy of finance is one sector of the commercial bourgeoisie.

Fixed and Circulating Capital: Fixed capital is constant capital invested in the instruments of production (buildings, tools, etc.) It is called fixed capital because it is not used up all at once in the production of the commodity; its value minus the costs of wear and tear remains "fixed" in the instruments of production. All other capital investment is circulating capital because it is completely consumed in one production cycle, and its value passes immediately into the commodity. (See Marx, *Capital*, vol. 2, chapter 8.)

Floating Relative Surplus Population. *See* SURPLUS POPULATION.

Force: Concept originally developed by Hegel in *The Phenomenology of Mind*. Hegel argued that the substance of the essence (as opposed to appearance) of reality is an interplay of energies. These energies or "forces" do not interact randomly but rather according to laws, which are the object of philosophy to discover. There is a conceptual continuity, albeit with definite changes of application, between the Hegelian concept of forces and the Marxian concept of the forces of production. *See also* MOTION AND FORCE.

Forces of Production: Marxian economic concept. The forces of production include both those factors which determine the given level of productivity of labor and what labor could potentially achieve if it were unfettered by irrational relations of production. The given level of productivity is the result of a multitude of different types of forces of production of which four are of special importance: (1) The instruments or the tools of labor increase the productivity of labor as they are developed; (2) As the skill level of labor develops, so does productivity; (3) The relations of production themselves can be a force of production to the extent that they provide an environment which drives productivity forward; (4) The motivation of labor to work affects productivity. The forces of production increase if people are enthusiastic and energetic about their work. They are then more likely to be creative in inventing new techniques as well as in utilizing the existing ones to their fullest capacity. The potential productivity of labor refers to what is in the process of becoming. Consequently the forces of production can also contain aspects which would pay off in future productivity, such as science and revolutionary activity which removed irrational class fetters to productivity.

See also CONTRADICTION; FORCE.

Foreign Market. *See* MARKET.

For Itself. *See* IN ITSELF AND FOR ITSELF.

Formation. *See* SOCIOECONOMIC FORMATION.

Freedom: "The control over ourselves and over external nature, a control founded on knowledge of natural necessity." Freedom "is therefore necessarily a product of historical development" (Engels, *Anti-Duhring*, p. 136). The Marxian concept of freedom is inextricably tied to the concept of necessity.

Hegel was the first to state correctly the relation between freedom and necessity. To him, freedom is the appreciation of necessity. "Necessity is *blind* only *in so far as it is not understood.*" Freedom does not consist in the dream of independence from natural laws, but in the knowledge of these laws, and in the possibility this gives of systematically making them work towards definite ends. This holds good in relation both to the laws of external nature and to those which govern the bodily and mental existence of men themselves—two classes of laws which we can separate from each other at most only in thought but not in reality. Freedom of the will therefore means nothing but the capacity to make decision with knowledge of the subject. Therefore the *freer* a man's judgment is in relation to a definite question, the greater is the *necessity* with which the content of this judgment will be determined; while the uncertainty, founded on ignorance, which seems to make an arbitrary choice among many different and conflicting possible decisions, shows precisely by this that it is not free, that it is controlled by the very object it should itself control. [*Ibid.*]

People are born into conditions that create the environment within which they can make choices. People are free to make choices within a certain *necessary* context. Marx wrote, "Men make their own history, but they do not make it just as they please; they do not make it under circumstances chosen by themselves, but under circumstances directly encountered, given and transmitted from the past" (*The Eighteenth Brumaire of Louis Bonaparte* p. 398). Finally, in contrast to the bourgeois concept which defines freedom as independence from others, the Marxian concept of freedom is collective. "Only within the community has each individual the means of cultivating his gifts in all directions; hence personal freedom becomes possible only within the community" (Marx and Engels, *The German Ideology*, p. 86). In contrast, the bourgeois concept of freedom "leads every man to see in other men, not the *realization*, but rather the *limitation* of his own liberty"(Marx, "On the Jewish Question").

Freedom and Necessity. *See* FREEDOM.

Free Labor: Labor that is formally able to sell its labor power to any employer. Free labor, i.e. that the worker can treat her or his own labor power as a commodity to be sold, is a distinguishing feature of capitalist societies.

Free Peasants. *See* SERFS AND FREE PEASANTS.

Fundamental Contradiction of Capitalism: Between the increasing socialization of production which requires social planning for its coordination and the continuance of private appropriation or fragmentary planning by individual capitalists only in accord with their own particular profit needs. A result of this contradiction is the tendency toward periodic economic crises.

G

General Form of Value: Type of exchange value equation analyzed by Marx in *Capital*, Chapter 1, Section 3 where the values of all commodities are expressed by how much of a single commodity set apart to which each is equivalent; for example, one peach, or one handkerchief, or one pen, etc., is worth the same in exchange value as one mango. The commodity that is set apart becomes the universal equivalent of the others, the standard against which all others are measured. When this form first historically achieves universality all commodities, with the exception of that which serves as the universal equivalent, become relative forms of value.

See ELEMENTARY FORM OF VALUE; EXCHANGE VALUE; EXPANDED FORM OF VALUE; MONEY; MONEY FORM OF VALUE; RELATIVE AND EQUIVALENT FORMS OF VALUE; UNIVERSAL EQUIVALENT.

General Law of Capitalist Accumulation: Law discovered by Marx that in capitalist societies capital growth and unemployment are functionally interrelated, i.e., capital growth requires the existence of unemployment. Marx wrote:

> the greater the social wealth, the functioning of capital, the extent and energy of its growth, and, therefore, also the absolute mass of the proletariat and the productiveness of its labor, the greater is the industrial reserve army. The same causes which develop the expansive power of capital, develop also the labor-power at its disposal. The relative mass of the industrial reserve army increases therefore with the potential energy of wealth. But the greater this reserve army in proportion to the active labor-army, the greater is the mass of a consolidated surplus-population, whose misery is in inverse ratio to its torment of labor. The more extensive, finally, the lazarus-layers of the working class, and the industrial reserve army, the greater is official pauperism. *This is the absolute general law of capitalist accumulation.* Like all other laws it is modified in its working by many circumstances. . . . [Marx, *Capital*, p. 603]

See also ACCUMULATION OF CAPITAL; INDUSTRIAL RESERVE ARMY; SURPLUS POPULATION.

General (Average) Rate of Profit and Surplus Profit: A measure that is based on the total surplus value produced in a country divided by the total amount of social capital invested in labor power and the means of production.

> The formation of the average rate of profit is, therefore, not merely a matter of obtaining the simple average of the different rates of profit in the various spheres of production, but rather one of the relative weight which these different rates of profit have in forming this average. This, however, depends on the relative magnitude of the capital invested in each particular sphere, or on the aliquot part which the capital invested in each particular sphere forms in the aggregate social capital. . . . The average rate of profit is determined by two factors: (1) The organic composition of the capitals in the different spheres of production, and thus, the different rates of profit in the individual spheres. (2) The distribution of the total social capital in these different spheres, and thus, the relative magnitude of the capital invested in each particular sphere at the specific rate of profit prevailing in it; i.e., the relative share of the total social capital absorbed by each individual sphere of production. [Marx, *Capital*, vol. 3, p. 162]

Surplus profit is profit above the average rate of profit. "Our analysis has revealed how the market-value . . . embraces a surplus-profit for those who produce in any particular sphere of production under the most favorable conditions" (Ibid., p. 198).

Gens (plural **Gentes**): A number of families united by a common blood descent. Gens is a synonym for *clan*.
See also GENS, PHRATRY, TRIBE, NATION.

Gens, Phratry, Tribe, Nation: Progressively more inclusive categories originally based on common descent and blood relationships. A gens (plural, gentes) was composed of the individuals descended from a common ancestor. Marx and Engels believed that the gentes were originally based on common female descent, but as father-right displaced mother-right, the gentes shifted to the basis of common male descent. The importance of the gens is that it was the unit of organization of primitive society. The monogamous family as a social unit of organization came only later. Thus, under gentile conditions the husband and wife belonged to different gentes while the children belonged either to the gens of the father or the mother depending on which system of common descent was in effect. Marx and Engels accepted the American anthropologist Lewis H. Morgan's conclusion that the gens was the unit of analysis for the Iroquois, Greeks, Romans, Scots, Irish, Germans, and others. The head of the gens was dominant over the head of the family.

Clan is sometimes used as a synonym for gens. A phratry was composed of several gentes while, originally, a tribe was composed of several phratries. "Just as several gentes constitute a phratry, so, in the classical form, several phratries constitute a tribe" (Engels, *The Origin of the Family, Private Property, and the State*, p. 90). The term tribe later was used to designate those living in the same territory; hence common territory displaced common descent as the basis of the term. Finally, a nation, in one of its forms, represents the coming together of two or more tribes.

Gentes: *See* GENS.

Gentile Constitution: The social organizational form that predated the state. The gentile constitution covered those who were members of the same gens, phratry, or tribe. Among its functions were provision for a common military (directed against external enemies), authority, and assembly. (See Engels, *The Origin of the Family, Private Property, and the State*, p. 103ff.)

Goal of Capitalism: The production of surplus value and accumulation of capital.

> The result of the capitalist production process is neither a mere product (use-value) nor a *commodity*, that is, a use-value which has a certain exchange-value. Its result, its product, is the creation of surplus-value for capital, and consequently the actual *transformation* of money or commodity into capital—which before the production process they were only in intention, in their essence, in what they were destined to be. In the production process more labor is absorbed than has been bought. This absorption, this *appropriation* of another's unpaid labor, which is consumated in the production process, is the *direct aim* of the capitalist production process; for what capital as capital (hence the capitalist as capitalist) wants to produce is neither an immediate use-value for individual consumption nor a commodity to be turned first into money and then into a use-value. Its aim is the *accumulation of wealth*, the *self-expansion of value*, *its increase*; that is to say, the maintenance of the old value and the creation of surplus-value. And it achieves this *specific* product of the capitalist production process only in exchange with labor, which for that reason is called *productive labor*. [Marx, *Theories of Surplus Value*, part 1, p. 399]

Gross Income: The total receipts of a business. Marx wrote that gross income is "equal to the total product or the value of the total product. (*Theories of Surplus Value*, part 2, p. 547).

Ground Rent: The sum of money or other goods paid by a tenant to a

landlord for the use of the land owned by the latter. Marx wrote in volume 3 of *Capital* (p. 618):

> The prerequisites for the capitalist mode of production therefore are the
> following: The actual tillers of the soil are wage-laborers employed by a
> capitalist, the capitalist farmer who is engaged in agriculture merely as a
> particular field of exploitation for capital, as investment for his capital in a
> particular sphere of production. This capitalist farmer pays the landowner,
> the owner of the land exploited by him, a sum of money at definite periods
> fixed by contract, for instance, annually (just as the borrower of money-
> capital pays a fixed interest), for the right to invest his capital in this specific
> sphere of production. This sum of money is called ground-rent, no matter
> whether it is paid for agricultural land, building lots, mines, fishing grounds,
> or forests, etc. It is paid for the entire time for which the landowner has
> contracted to rent his land to the capitalist farmer. Ground-rent, therefore,
> is here that form in which property in land is realized economically, that is,
> produces value.

In Marx's analysis, ground rent is one of the component parts of surplus
value—the other two important parts are interest and profit. There are
three analytical categories in Marx's theory of ground rent, or the
interest that the land user pays to the landowner. Marx's definitions were
analytical, that is, they defined the economic reasons for the varying
sizes of the component parts of ground-rent. *Total* (sometimes also
called *actual*) *ground rent* equals the market value of what is produced
on the land minus the market value of the capital invested in its production (plus a profit which is equal to the average profit on capital investments of equal magnitudes in the economy as a whole). The existence of
ground rent presupposes land monopolization to some degree and thus
the possibility of excess profits on investments, i.e. profits above the
prevailing average for the economy as a whole and therefore large
enough to cover both the average profit and a rent. Total rent, derived
from these excess profits, has two component parts: absolute and differential ground rent. *Absolute ground rent* equals that portion of excess
profits that comes from the differences between the value of the produce
of the least productive land in cultivation and the market value of the
capital invested in its production (plus a profit which is equal to the
average profit on capital investments of equal magnitudes in the economy as a whole). Absolute ground rent existed because of the low
organic composition of capital invested in agriculture relative to the
organic compositions of other spheres of production in Marx's time.
In the case of the early industrial stage of capitalist development,
the organic composition of capital was lower in agriculture than in
industry and hence yielded higher profits (i.e., there was a relatively

greater proportion of labor power to be exploited) which enabled the existence of absolute ground rent. *Differential ground rent* is equal to the value of the produce on more productive lands (e.g., more fertile or closer to the market) under cultivation minus the value of the produce of the least productive lands under cultivation. Differential rent "is nothing but surplus profit, which exists also in every sphere of industrial production for any capital which is put to work under conditions better than the average. The only thing is that in agriculture it gets firmly established because it is based on so solid and (relatively) firm a foundation as the different degrees of natural fertility of different types of soil" (*Letters*, Marx to Engels, August 2, 1862).

Group Marriage: "The form in which whole groups of men and whole groups of women belong to one another" (Engels, *The Origin of the Family, Private Property and the State*, p. 36). Group marriage was an early stage in the development of the family which corresponded to the period of savagery.
See also SAVAGERY.

Guild: An association within feudal towns of people who performed the same craft. The guilds regulated prices, suppressed competition among members, and regulated entrance into the crafts through elaborate apprenticeship systems.
See also APPRENTICE; CRAFT; FEUDALISM; JOURNEYMAN; MASTER.

H

Hetaerism: Greek term for nonmarital sexual relations.

This word was used by the Greeks, when they introduced it, to describe intercourse between unmarried men, or those living in monogamy, and unmarried women; it always presupposed the existence of a definite form of marriage outside of which this intercourse takes place, and includes prostitution, at least as an already existing possibility. The word was never used in any other sense and I use it in this sense with Morgan. [Engels, *The Origin of the Family, Private Property, and the State*, p. 32]

Historical Contradiction. *See* CONTRADICTION.

Historical Materialism: The scientific method developed by Marx and Engels. They provided several descriptions of its basic elements. (1) ". . . that view of the course of history which seeks the ultimate cause and the great moving power of all important historic events in the economic development of society, in the changes in the modes of production and exchange, in the consequent division of society into distinct classes, and in the struggles of these classes against one another" (Engels, 1892 Introduction to "Socialism: Utopian and Scientific," p. 103). (2) Historical materialism is often briefly described as the application of dialectical materialism to the study of history. (3) "Just as Darwin discovered the law of development of organic nature, so Marx discovered the law of development of human history; the simple fact, hitherto concealed by an overgrowth of ideology, that mankind must first of all eat, drink, have shelter and clothing, before it can pursue politics, science, art, religion, etc: that therefore the production of the immediate material means of subsistence and consequently the degree of economic development attained by a given people or during a given epoch form the foundation upon which the state institutions, the legal conceptions, art, and even the ideas on religion, of the people concerned have been evolved, and in the light of which they must, therefore, be explained, instead of *vice versa*, as had hiterto been the case." (Engels, "Speech at the Graveside of Karl Marx", p. 162).

According to the materialist conception of history, the *ultimately* determining element of history is the production and reproduction of real life. More than this neither Marx nor I have ever asserted. Hence if somebody twists this into saying that the economic element is the *only* determining one, he transforms that proposition into a meaningless, abstract, senseless phrase. The economic situation is the basis, but the various elements of the superstructure—political forms of the class struggle and its results, to wit: constitutions established by the victorious class after a successful battle, etc., juridical forms, and even the reflexes of all these actual struggles in the brains of the participants, political, juristic, philosophical theories, religious views and their further development into systems of dogmas—also exercise their influence upon the course of the historical struggles and in many case preponderate in determining their *form*. There is an interaction of all these elements in which, amid all the endless host of accidents (that is, of things and events whose inner interconnection is so remote or so impossible of proof that we can regard it as nonexistent, as negligible), the economic movement finally asserts itself as necessary. [Letters, Engels to J. Bloch, September 21, 1890]

(4)

The materialist conception of history starts from the proposition that the production of the means to support human life and, next to production, the exchange of things produced, is the basis of all social structure; that in every society that has appeared in history, the manner in which wealth is distributed and society divided into classes or orders is dependent upon what is produced, how it is produced, and how the products are exchanged. From this point of view the final causes of all social changes and political revolutions are to be sought, not in man's better insight into eternal truth and justice, but in changes in the modes of production and exchange. They are to be sought, not in the *philosophy*, but in the *economics* of each particular epoch. The growing perception that existing social institutions are unreasonable and unjust, that reason has become unreason, and right wrong, is only proof that in the modes of production and exchange changes have silently taken place with which the social order, adapted to earlier economic conditions, is no longer in keeping. From this it also follows that the means of getting rid of the incongruities that have been brought to light must also be present, in a more or less developed condition, within the changed modes of production themselves. These means are not to be *invented*, spun out of the head, but *discovered* with the aid of the head in the existing material facts of production. [Engels, *Anti-Duhring*, p. 316]

(5)

This conception of history thus relies on expounding the real process of production—starting from the material production of life itself—and comprehending the form of intercourse connected with and created by this mode of production, i.e., civil society in its various stages, as the basis of all history; describing it in its action as the state, and also explaining how all the different theoretical products and forms of consciousness, religion, philosophy, morality, etc., etc., arise from it, and tracing the process of their formation from that basis; thus the whole thing can, of course, be depicted in its totality (and therefore, too, the reciprocal action of these various sides on one another). It has not, like the idealist view of history, to look for a category in every period, but remains constantly on the real *ground* of history; it doesn't explain practice from the ideal but explains the formation of ideas from material practice, and accordingly it comes to the conclusion that all forms and products of consciousness cannot be dissolved by mental criticism, by resolution into "self-consciousness" or transformation into "apparitions", "spectres", "whimsies", etc., but only by the practical overthrow of the actual social relations which gave rise to this idealistic humbug; that not criticism but revolution is the driving force of history, also of religion, of philosophy and all other kinds of theory. It shows that history does not end by being resolved into "self-consciousness" as "spirit of the spirit", but that each stage contains a material result, a sum of productive forces, a historically created relation to nature and of individuals to one another, which is handed down to each generation from its predecessor; a mass of productive forces, capital funds and circumstances, which on the one hand is indeed modified by the new generation, but on the other also prescribes for its conditions of life and gives it a definite development, a special character. It shows that circumstances make men just as much as men make circumstances. This sum of productive forces, capital funds and social forms of intercourse, which every individual and every generation finds in existence as something given, is the real basis of what the philosophers have conceived as "substance" and "essence of man", and what they have deified and attacked; a real basis which is not in the least disturbed, in its effect and influence on the development of men, but the fact that these philosophers revolt against it as "self-consciousness" and the "unique". These conditions of life, which different generations find in existence, determine also whether or not the revolutionary convulsion periodically recurring in history will be strong enough to overthrow the basis of everything that exists. And if these material elements of a complete revolution are not present—namely, on the one hand the existing productive forces, on the other the formation of a revolutionary mass, which revolts not only against separate conditions of the existing society, but against the existing "production of life" itself, the "total activity" on which it was based—then it is absolutely immaterial for practical development whether the *idea* of this revolution has been expressed a hundred times already, as the history of communism proves. [Marx and Engels, *The German Ideology*, pp. 61-62]

Historical Specification: Marxist methodological principle that an object of analysis must be interpreted within the context of its own particular historical period. A mode of production or type of society such as capitalism, feudalism, or communism coheres with and gives meaning to a distinct and particular set of social relations. Hence those relations cannot be interpreted according to the preconceptions of another historical period nor can they be interpreted abstractly as transhistorical.

History: Branch of knowledge which deals with the development of human societies over time. "History is nothing but the succession of the separate generations, each of which uses the materials, the capital funds, the productive forces handed down to it by all preceding generations, and thus, on the one hand, continues the traditional activity in completely changed circumstances and, on the other, modifies the old circumstances with a completely changed activity" (Marx and Engels, *The German Ideology*, p. 58).

> Just as knowledge is unable to reach a complete conclusion in a perfect, ideal condition of humanity, so is history unable to do so; a perfect society, a perfect "state," are things which can only exist in imagination. On the contrary, all successive historical systems are only transitory stages in the endless course of development of human society from the lower to the higher. Each stage is necessary, and therefore justified for the time and conditions to which it owes its origin. But in the fact of new, higher conditions which gradually develop in its own womb, it loses its validity and justification. It must give way to a higher stage which will also in its turn decay and perish. [Engels, *Ludwig Feuerbach and the End of Classical German Philosophy*, p. 339]

History Dialectic. *See* NATURE AND HISTORY DIALECTIC.

Home Market. *See* MARKET.

House Rent: Sum that a tenant pays for the use of a house owned by another.

> . . . house rent is composed as follows: (1) a part which is ground rent; (2) a part which is interest on the building capital, including the profit of the builder; (3) a part which goes for repairs and insurance; (4) a part which has to amortise the building capital inclusive of profit in annual deductions according to the rate at which the house gradually depreciates. . . . If we then deduct from the total rent paid for the house the following: (1) the ground rent together with any increase it may have experienced during the period in question, and (2) the sums expended for current repairs, we shall find that the remainder is composed on an average as follows: (1) the building capital originally invested in the house, (2) the profit on this, and (3) the interest on the gradually maturing capital and profit. [Engels, "The Housing Question," p. 321]

Human Nature. *See* SPECIES-BEING.

Husbandry: Farming, including the tilling of the soil and domestication of animals.

Hypothesis: A statement of a possible relationship which is yet to be verified by investigation.

Idea, the: Hegelian concept meaning generally God's will or divine purpose in history.

> In contemplating world history we must thus consider its ultimate purpose. This ultimate purpose is what is willed in the world itself. We know of God that He is the most perfect; He can will only Himself and what is like Him. God and the nature of His will are one and the same; these we call, philosophically, the Idea. Hence, it is the Idea in general, in its manifestation as human spirit, which we have to contemplate. More precisely, it is the idea of human freedom. The purest form in which the Idea manifests itself is Thought itself. In this aspect the Idea is treated in Logic. Another form is that of physical Nature. The third form, finally, is that of Spirit in general. [Hegel, *Reason in History*, p. 21]

Idealism: Adherence to philosophies which uphold the premise that ideas are logically prior to material things in reality. There are several schools of idealism varying in the degree to which they emphasize the primacy of ideas. Kant's critical idealism for example posited that the objects of perception as known to us consist in our ideas of them. The objects exist outside our ideas but we can only know them as filtered through our ideas of them. Hegel's absolute idealism on the other hand posited that the objects themselves were manifestations of ideas. The distinguishing premise of idealism thus is that all knowledge and consciousness are subjectively generated. The Marxian and philosophical concept of idealism is different from a popular meaning that the term has since acquired. In the popular meaning an idealist is someone who is motivated by idealized, somewhat unpractical principles.

Ideology: Generically, the *logos* (Greek), or knowledge of ideas. The term was introduced by Napoleon as a slur against impractical intellectuals. Since then, it has acquired a number of different meanings and usages, some of which creep into Marxian discourse. (1) Popularly, ideology refers to any set of political ideas, valid or invalid. The term is sometimes used by Marxists in this manner today. (2) Within Western sociology there are three different uses of the term. (*a*) Ideology is used as a term to describe the overall idea structure of a society, that is, those ideas that tend to be held in common and guide a society. (*b*) Ideology is used as a term to describe the views of extremist groups which are the result of a faulty societal integration. (*c*) In a usage which approximates the Marxian, ideology refers to sets of ideas that further the interests of particular groups or classes. (3) Marx used the term to mean the set of ideas which expressed the interests of the ruling class. Ruling-class ideology is a falsifying partial view though because (*a*) it expresses their particular interests rather than the interests of society as a whole, and (*b*) self-interest blinds members of the ruling class from seeing the historical necessity of their destruction as a class. Consciousness and science are counterposed to ideology. The former are total dialectical views while the latter is partial. Ideology ends with the end of class society and its generated contradictory world views due to antagonistic class contradictions and interests.

Immanent: The operation of forces totally inherent or internal to something that is in the process of development.

In Itself and For Itself: Concepts of dialectical logic. The *in itself* and *for itself* terminology that has been applied most prominently in class analysis is Hegelian in origin. In itself (*an sich* in German) meant latent or unconscious while for itself (*fur sich*), the antithesis of in itself, means consciously. "With Hegel, 'in itself' contains the distinction and separation of these hidden elements and the starting point of their conflict" (Engels, *Anti-Duhring*, p. 74).
See also CLASS.

Individual and Social Capital: Terms used by Marx to distinguish between the capital owned by individual interests and that which had accumulated in the society as a whole. In later Marxist writing, the term *social capital* is sometimes used to indicate capital that is employed by the state as distinct from privately owned and controlled capital. Marx also used social capital to indicate the combined capital of more than one capitalist in an undertaking.

Individual Consumption. *See* PRODUCTIVE AND INDIVIDUAL CONSUMPTION.

Individual, Particular, Universal: Dialectical categories used to express the differences and similarities of objects. Objects are different, hence they have *individuality*. But at the same time they share certain features.

If the shared feature is common only to a similar group of objects, it is the *particularity* of that group; if the shared feature is common to all objects, it is a *universal.*

Industrial Bourgeoisie: The sector of the capitalist class that specializes in the production as opposed to the circulation of commodities.

Industrial Reserve Army. *See* RELATIVE SURPLUS POPULATION.

Industrial Revolution: The period between roughly 1780 and 1820 when a number of technical inventions (e.g. the steam engine, steamship, and locomotive engine) paved the way for substituting mechanical for human energy in the production process.

Industry. *See* INDUSTRY AND MANUFACTURING.

Industry and Manufacturing: Marx's division of factories into two types which occurred generally as successive stages. Manufacturing is factory work based on manual work and human energy. Industry is factory work that employs machines and nonhuman sources of energy such as steam, electricity, oil, and so on. In bourgeois political economy "all industry, not agricultural or handicraft, is indiscriminately comprised in the term of manufacture, and thereby the distinction is obliterated between two great and essentially different periods of economic history: the period of manufacture proper, based on the division of manual labor, and the period of modern industry based on machinery" (Engels, Preface to the English edition of *Capital*, p. 15).

Instruments of Labor: One of the three functional parts of production. "The elementary factors of the labor-process are 1, the personal activity of man, i.e., work itself, 2, the subject of that work, and 3, its instruments" (Marx, *Capital*, p. 174). In particular, "An instrument of labor is a thing, or a complex of things, which the laborer interposes between himself and the subject of his labor, and which serves as the conductor of his activity. He makes use of the mechanical, physical, and chemical properties of some substances in order to make other substances subservient to his aims" (ibid.). We can thus say that the instruments of labor include such things as tools, baskets, and domesticated animals which people use to produce. But the instruments of labor are still more inclusive.

> In a wider sense we may include among the instruments of labor, in addition to those things that are used for directly transferring labor to its subject,

and which therefore, in one way or another, serve as conductors of activity, all such objects as are necessary for carrying on the labor-process. These do not enter directly into the process, but without them it is either impossible for it to take place at all, or possible only to a partial extent. Once more we find the earth to be a universal instrument of this sort, for it furnishes a locus standi to the laborer and a field of employment for his activity. Among instruments that are the result of previous labor and also belong to this class, we find workshops, canals, roads, and so forth. [ibid., p. 176]

The above mentioned elementary factors of the labor process-labor power, the subject of the work (i.e., that which is to be worked upon in order to transform it), and the instruments of labor—are defined not according to their individual concrete identities as for example worker, tool, or wood, but rather in accord with their *function* within the production process. ". . . whether a use-value is to be regarded as raw material, as instrument of labor, or as product, this is determined entirely by its function in the labor-process, by the position it there occupies: as this varies, so does its character" (ibid., p. 178).

Intercourse: Used in a wide sense by Marx and Engels in *The German Ideology* to indicate all of the material and ideal interrelationships within and between societies.

Interest: The amount of money which is charged to a borrower for a loan. Marx was particularly interested in the interest payments made by industrial capitalists. In that case interest was a part of the profit. "Interest . . . appears originally, is originally, and remains in fact merely a portion of the profit, i.e., of the surplus-value, which the functioning capitalist, industrialist or merchant has to pay to the owner and lender of money-capital whenever he uses loaned capital instead of his own." (Marx, *Capital*, vol. 3, p. 370) Marx demonstrated that interest is one of the parts into which the general quantity of societal surplus value is divided—the other two are profit and rent.

Interest-bearing Capital: That part of capital which is used solely for loans. Interest-bearing capital is a part of money capital which is controlled by banks, loan agencies, and the like.

J

Joint-stock Company: Nineteenth-century term used by Marx to indicate companies which attracted the capitals of more than one capitalist by selling shares in the company ownership. This development furthered the concentration and centralization of capital. Today a joint-stock company would be called a corporation.

Journeyman: Classification in the feudal shop for those who had served the period of apprenticeship in order to learn the particular trade or craft but who still had to finish serving a period as an employee of a master. *See also* APPRENTICE; FEUDALISM; GUILD; MASTER.

K

Kantianism and Neo-Kantianism: Tendencies in the philosophy of science based on an interpretation of the philosophy of Immanual Kant. The aspect of Kant's philosophy which was most influential for the neo-Kantians was his distinction between phenomena and noumena. The distinction is also known as that between form and content and between the qualities of a thing and the thing-in-itself (the *Ding an sich*). Kant postulated that human capability was limited to only knowing the outward appearance or phenomena of things and not the thing-in-itself. Human beings perceive through categories internal to their minds. Hence what they perceive, the phenomenon, is a filtered version of the thing-in-itself. The neo-Kantians took over this view and made it a premise of their philosophy of science. The result was a scientific and in some areas social agnosticism. Engels, however, refuted this view.

> But then come the Neo-Kantian agnostics and say: We may correctly perceive the qualities of a thing, but we cannot by any sensible or mental process grasp the thing-in-itself. This "thing-in-itself" is beyond our ken. To this Hegel, long since, has replied: If you know all the qualities of a thing, you know the thing itself; nothing remains but the fact that the said exists without us; and when your senses have taught you that fact, you have grasped the last remnant of the thing-in-itself, Kant's celebrated unknowable *Ding an sich*. To which it may be added that in Kant's time our knowledge of natural objects was indeed so fragmentary that he might well suspect, behind the little we knew about each of them, a mysterious "thing-in-itself". But one after another these ungrasperable things have been grasped, analyzed, and, what is more, *reproduced* by the giant progress of science; and what we can produce we certainly cannot consider as unknowable. [Engels, "Socialism: Utopian and Scientific," p. 102]

> The most telling refutation of this as of all other philosophical crotchets is practice, namely, experiment and industry. If we are able to prove the correctness of our conception of a natural process by making it ourselves, bringing it into being out of its conditions and making it serve our own purposes into the bargain, then there is an end to the Kantian ungraspable "thing-in-itself." [Engels, *Ludwig Feuerbach and the End of Classical German Philosophy*, p. 347]

L

Labor: Physical and/or mental exertion in production.

> Labor is, in the first place, a process in which both man and Nature participate, and in which man of his own accord starts, regulates, and controls the material re-actions between himself and Nature. He opposes himself to Nature as one of her own forces, setting in motion arms and legs, head and hands, the natural forces of his body, in order to appropriate Nature's productions in a form adapted to his own wants. By thus acting on the external world and changing it, he at the same time changes his own nature. He develops his slumbering powers and compels them to act in obedience to his sway. [Marx, *Capital*, p. 173]

The concept of labor is central to Marxism. Marx considered the nature of human labor to be one of the two distinguishing characteristics of human nature—the other was that humans are social beings. Human labor is creative and is thus distinct from animal labor which is instinctual. How human labor has developed, been organized, and been controlled is a central thread to history.

See also CONCRETE AND ABSTRACT LABOR; COOPERATIVE LABOR; CREATIVE LABOR; DIVISION OF LABOR; ELEMENTARY FACTORS OF THE LABOR PROCESS; FREE LABOR; INSTRUMENTS OF LABOR; LABORER; LABOR POWER; LABOR THEORY OF VALUE; LIVING AND DEAD LABOR; NECESSARY AND SURPLUS LABOR; PRODUCT OF LABOR; PRODUCTIVE LABOR; SELF-ESTRANGEMENT OF LABOR; SOCIAL LABOR; SOCIALLY NECESSARY LABOR-TIME; SUBJECT OF LABOR; VALUE OF LABOR.

Labor Aristocracy: Concept originally developed by Engels to describe the relatively privileged position *vis-à-vis* the rest of the working class of skilled tradesmen and top trade union officials. The position of relative privilege was the social basis for a tendency to pursue a politics of narrow self-interest rather than class interest—that is, a politics of opportunism. Lenin later made the concept of a labor aristocracy a key part of his theory of imperialism. The labor aristocracies of the imperialist countries shared in the super-profits extracted from the oppressed colonies and thus were "bribed" to support the foreign activities of their respective bourgeoisies, according to Lenin's theory.

Labor Market: Term used to describe the overall buying and selling of labor power in capitalist societies. Most rates of wages and salaries are set in accordance with market principles.

Labor Power: The physical and/or mental capacity to work which the worker sells to capital in exchange for wages or a salary.

Labor Theory of Value: Marx's theory that the exchange values of commodities are set by the relative amounts of social labor incorporated in their production. Marx wrote, "the value of a commodity, therefore, varies directly as the quantity, and inversely as the productiveness, of the labor incorporated in it" (*Capital*, p. 48). There are two parts of the labor theory of value that need to be understood in order to avoid an incorrect impression. First, labor means *social* labor, i.e., the quantity of labor corresponding to current standards of productivity. Thus the extra labor time taken by an inefficient or lazy worker is not productive of exchange value. Second, skilled labor is more productive than unskilled labor. The labor theory of value is one of the fundamental premises of Marxian economics. On its basis Marx deducted the inevitable exploitation of workers in capitalist societies and the parasitic role of capitalists. Bourgeois economics counters by arguing that the role of capitalists is also productive of value.

Laborer: General term for anyone who works in any mode of production in a subordinate position—slaves, workers, or peasants. *Laborer* as such is not a class term because it does not designate any particular class. It is rather a status term, i.e., it designates a relative position within a hierarchy.

Land Capital: Land that yields interest to the owner. "The representative of land as capital is not the landlord, but the farmer. The proceeds yielded by land as capital are interest and industrial profit, not rent. There are lands which yield such interest and profit but still yield no rent. Briefly, land in so far as it yields interest, is land capital, and as land capital it yields no rent, it is not landed property" (Marx, *The Poverty of Philosophy*, p. 143).

Landlord Class: Feudal class based on the ownership or control of large amounts of land which was not utilized chiefly for commodity production. The landlord's source of income was ground rent in kind or money. In the early stages of capitalist development the landlords continued to receive their income from ground rent, though the land began to be used for commodity production. In later stages of capitalist developments the landlords merged with and became a sector of the capitalist class. *See also* FEUDALISM; GROUND RENT.

Latent Relative Surplus Population. *See* SURPLUS POPULATION.

Law: Formalized rule with sanctions enforced by a state.

> At a certain, very primitive stage of the development of society, the need arises to bring under a common rule the daily recurring acts of production, distribution and exchange of products, to see to it that the individual subordinates himself to the common conditions of production and exchange. This rule, which at first is custom, soon becomes *law*. With law, organs necessarily arise which are entrusted with its maintenance—public authority, the state. With further social development, law develops into a more or less comprehensive legal system. The more intricate this legal system becomes, the more is its mode of expression removed from that in which the usual economic conditions of the life of society are expressed. It appears as an independent element which derives the justification for its existence and the substantiation of its further development not from the economic relations but from its own inner foundations or, if you like, from "the concept of the will." People forget that their right derived from their economic conditions of life, just as they have forgotten that they themselves derive from the animal world. [Engels, "The Housing Question," p. 365]

Law of Identity: Law in formal logic that A = A and cannot = non-A. Dialectical logic, to the contrary, sees a large part of the identity of *A* being made up by what it is not.

Laws of Dialectics: Engels listed three laws of dialectics from the work of Hegel, which he stated were applicable to both nature and history:

(1) The universality of change and the transformation of quantity to quality. The law states briefly that change in history and nature is incremental up to a certain nodal point and then the incremental change results in producing a qualitative change that transforms the identity of that which is being changed. "The straw that broke the camel's back" is a popular saying that exemplifies the law. An example from nature is the transformation of water to steam when incremental increases in temperature pass a certain degree. An example from history is the transformation of feudalism to capitalism. Commodity production increased to the point that the social system could no longer be characterized as feudalism; it had become capitalism. Marx wrote, "You will also see from the conclusion of my Chapter III (Capital), where the transformation of the handicraft-master into a capitalist—as a result of merely *quantitative*

changes—is touched upon, that *in that text* I refer to Hegel's discovery—
the *law of merely quantitative changes turning into qualitative changes*—
as holding good alike in history and natural science" (Letters, Marx to
Engels, June 22, 1867). Change is thus not linear in history. For example,
a society does not simply become more technologically efficient and
modern through history. There are rather thresholds or nodal points in
historical development after which the society has changed to the point
where a new category is required to describe it and its internal relations.

(2) The law of the mutual penetration of polar opposites and transformation into each other when carried to extremes has three interrelated
parts. (*a*) Contradiction is at the base of the development and movement
of all processes. The contradiction or struggle of opposites is the dyna-
mism that accounts for motion. For example, the fundamental contradiction that accounts for development of history is the contradiction
between the forces and relations of production. (*b*) The contradictory
aspects are not frozen separate identities; rather they "mutually penetrate" each other. A process can be understood only by identifying its
contradictory aspects and then by establishing their interrelationship
with each other. This part of the law is directed against the Aristotelian
law of identity of traditional logic which states that A equals A and that
A cannot equal not-A. If A equals A and nothing else, what is neglected
is that a good part of the identity of A is derived from its relationship to
the not-A's. For example, in personality development, much is incorporated from the personalities of others. In economics, the existence of
monopolies is dependent on the existence of competitive industries.
The term *monopoly* is relational in the sense that its meaning implies
what it is (control of the market) and what it is not (controlled by the
market). If the "what is not" no longer exists, then new terms have to be
developed in order to identify the phenomenon properly. Similarly, in
sociology, the meaning that there is a working class is that there is also
one or more classes that do not perform the same activity. It thus would
not make sense to speak of a society composed of one class alone; the
term *class* implies the existence of at least two classes in a society since
each class's meaning is as much determined by the class or classes that
it is not as by its own individuated identity. (*c*) Opposite aspects of the
contradiction can transform "into each other when carried to extremes."
That is, since each aspect of the contradiction carries in latent form the
other aspect as a part of its identity, in extremes the latent form can
develop into predominance. For example, the initially revolutionary
ideology of the rising bourgeoisie, Reason, turned into its opposite and
became a reactionary mask for status quo relations. With the capitalist
class contradiction the working class transforms itself from being the

oppressed class to its opposite after a revolution and the establishment of the dictatorship of the proletariat.

(3) The law of the negation of the negation or spiral form of development is a law which sums up the interconnections of developmental processes in nature, history, and ideas. Engels specifically claimed universality for the law: "When I say that all these processes (in nature, history, and thought) are a negation of the negation, I bring them all together under one law of motion. . ." (*Anti-Duhring*, p. 168). The law of the negation of the negation is an expression of the thesis-antithesis-synthesis triad of Hegelian dialects. Stated abstractly, the beginning development of a contradiction characterizes the first thesis stage. This originating general contradiction will underlie the whole process of development. The transformation of quantitative growth of the contradiction into a qualitative negation of the thesis characterizes the second antithesis stage of development. The antithesis represents a one-sided partial—though necessary—solution to the originating contradiction. The solutions established by this stage unleashed their own particular contradictions which add to the only partially resolved general contradiction of the first stage. This complex of contradictions provokes the negation of the antithesis stage, the negation of the negation. The result is a new synthesis which incorporates aspects of both the thesis and the antithesis. The new synthesis sublates aspects of the original thesis, that is, incorporates them but at a higher level. The original contradiction is resolved. In place of this contradiction a more advanced type of contradiction forms with the new synthesis which will provoke a new developmental process. The thesis-antithesis-synthesis triad or development of the negation of the negation represents not quite a cycle in the return to the sublated original thesis because it is now at a higher level; a spiral rather than a cycle is a more accurate pictorial metaphor for the process—hence, the "spiral form of development." Marx, for example, represented the process of history as moving from common property systems (the primitive communism stage) to their negation which are private property systems (slavery, feudalism, and capitalism) to the negation of the negation, which is communism. Communism is a return to and sublation at a higher stage of the original common property stage.

See also ABSTRACTION; CONCEPT; DIALECTICS; DIALECTICAL MATERIALISM; ESSENCE AND APPEARANCE; NODAL POINT; SUBLATE; THESIS-ANTITHESIS-SYNTHESIS.

Living and Dead Labor: Marx termed what labor had produced as materialized or dead labor, and labor in the act of production as living labor. In this sense the means of production and capital in general are dead labor; thus in the act of production living labor confronts dead labor. Dead labor is also called *congealed labor.*

Lower Middle Class. *See* MIDDLE CLASS.

Lumpenproletariat: From the German *lumpen* meaning "rag," that is literally, the "rag proletariat." The lumpenproletariat in Marx's and Engels's writings seemed to consist of two parts: the petty criminal population and the hobo population. Both parts are an omnipresent feature of capitalist societies and live outside of the labor force. An important distinguishing characteristic seems to be an intentional motivation that distinguishes them from the unemployed part of the labor force. Marx described at one point the French lumpenproletariat as "vagabonds, discharged soldiers, discharged jailbirds, escaped galley slaves, swindlers, mountebanks, *lazzaroni*, porters, literati, organ-grinders, rag pickers, knife grinders, tinkers, beggars. . ." (*The Eighteenth Brumaire of Louis Bonaparte*, p. 442). Various theorists from Marx's and Engels's times to the present have found in the lumpenproletariat a revolutionary vanguard because, so it is argued, they generally live outside the law and are thus least integrated into the normal workings of capitalist society. Marx and Engels from both theory and experience firmly rejected this view of the revolutionary potential of the lumpenproletariat. Rather, they argued, the lumpenproletariat's adopted way of life made them unusually susceptible to becoming bribed agents of the state. In later revolutionary struggles the lumpenproletariat have played both progressive and reactionary roles depending on the struggle. Mao, among others, thought that lumpen elements, if disciplined by the revolutionary organization, could play a valuable—though not leading, part in the struggle.

M

Machine: Composite tool driven by an energy source.

> The machine is a unification of the instruments of labor. . . . Simple tools; accumulation of tools; composite tools; setting in motion of a composite tool by a single hand engine, by man; setting in motion of these instruments by natural forces, machines; system of machines having one motor; system of machines having one automatic motor—this is the progress of machinery. [Marx, *The Poverty of Philosophy*, p. 120]

Malthusianism and Neo-Malthusianism: Ideas based on the arguments of Thomas Robert Malthus, a late-eighteenth and early-nineteenth century parson and political economist who forecast that the rate of population growth proceeded *geometrically* while that of food production at best only *arithmetically*—in other words, that population growth would outstrip the world's resources portending disaster. The basic theses of the neo-Malthusians are: First, because the rate of population is growing at a staggering rate the earth, will be grossly overpopulated in the not too distant future, and there will not be enough resources to support everyone. Second, overpopulation is the root cause of a large number of social problems such as poverty, hunger, riots, and even communism. Third, the problem of overpopulation is concentrated in the poor countries and domestically in minority and poor communities. Fourth, in order to cope with the threat of overpopulation, an aggressive program of population control is necessary. Marxists respond that the problem is not the ratio of people to food but rather how the distribution of food is organized that is the main cause of hunger; that science applied to agriculture makes it as productive as necessary to sustain the growth of population; that population growth rates are dependent on a number of social and economic factors; and finally that the neo-Malthusian argument is an ideological attempt to shift the blame for poverty from the nature of the class society to the poor themselves.

Manager: An employee who performs the function of supervising, controlling, and coordinating labor as an agent of the capitalist class.

Manifestation. *See* ESSENCE AND APPEARANCE.

Manufacturing. *See* INDUSTRY AND MANUFACTURING.

Market: General concept for the arenas where commoditties are bought and sold. Marx and Engels distinguished different types of markets. The *domestic market* is the market for commodities that can be sold for consumption within a household. In the early days of capitalist development, households produced much of what they consumed, for example, by making their own clothing or by keeping a garden. Hence, a domestic market was correspondingly restricted. But capitalism gradually captured the domestic market with mass production of, for example, cheap clothing. The *home market* is the market that exists within the confines of one's own territory, nation, or state. The *foreign market* is the market that exists for one's products outside the confines of one's own territory, nation, or state. The *colonial market* is the market that exists inside a colony for the goods produced in the country that controls the colony. For example, India was a colonial market for England's goods during the nineteenth century; Puerto Rico is a colonial market for the goods of the United States today. The *world market* is simply the summation of all existing markets.
See also COMMODITY MARKET; LABOR MARKET; MARKET PRICE.

Market Price: The empirical price of a particular commodity. Prices can and usually do fluctuate above and below the actual exchange value of the commodity, which expresses the relative amount of labor incorporated in its production. Market prices are thus influenced by but not the same as exchange values.

Mass of Profit. *See* RATE AND MASS OF PROFIT.

Master: The owner of the feudal shop, who was qualified to train apprentices in a particular trade or craft.
See also APPRENTICE; CRAFT; FEUDALISM; GUILD; JOURNEYMAN.

Material Conditions of Life: The totality of relations that people have to enter into in order to produce and reproduce what is necessary in order to live. The material conditions of life include both what is given by nature and what humanity does through labor to alter nature for its own needs. (See Marx, Preface to *A Contribution to the Critique of Political Economy*.)

Materialism: Philosophic premise about the nature of reality. The term has acquired several distinct meanings in its history. (1) Mechanical materialism is the view that nothing exists except matter and its motion and that all ideas are a direct reflection of the material world. (2) Popularly, materialism is identified with the view that humans have an innate psychological mechanism that causes them to be motivated only by hedonistic self-gain. "By the word materialism the Philistine understands gluttony, drunkenness, lust of the eye, lust of the flesh, arrogance, cupidity, avarice, covetousness, profit-hunting and stock-exchange swindling—in short, all the filthy vices in which he himself indulges in private" (Engels, *Ludwig Feuerbach and the End of Classical German Philosophy*, p. 353). (3) Marxian materialism is distinct from both the mechanical and popular conceptions. Marxian materialism is the premise that the basis of human existence is the activity which has been and must be done to sustain life. Such activity is the most powerful, though not exclusive, determinant of consciousness and social development. Marx rejected the mechanical meaning of materialism because it denied the role of consciousness as an intergal part of human activity. He rejected the popular meaning of materialism because he did not believe that human motivation was innately based on self-gain. Rather, he concluded that human beings had good or bad characteristics according to the situation; the point of socialism is to create a social structure in which the best qualities of human beings will be encouraged.

See also DIALECTICAL MATERIALISM; HISTORICAL MATERIALISM; MATERIAL CONDITIONS OF LIFE; MATTER; MECHANICAL MATERIALISM.

Matter: "Corporeally existing things" (Engels, *Anti-Duhring*, p. 445). Matter is thus to be contradistinguished from ideas, spirit, soul, or any other noncorporeal substance. "Matter is nothing but the totality of material things" (Engels, *Dialectics of Nature*, p. 312). Hegel had earlier written that "the essence of matter is gravity. . ." (Hegel, *Reason in History*, p. 22).

Means of Production: The factors that labor uses to produce the necessities and wealth of a particular form of society. Marx listed as means of production raw materials, auxiliary materials, and the instruments of labor. He also added the subject of labor, i.e., what labor was working upon to transform into a product. "If we examine the whole process from the point of view of its result, the product, it is plain that both the instruments and the subject of labor, are means of production. . . . It appears paradoxical to assert, that uncaught fish, for instance, are a means of production in the fishing industry. But hitherto no one has discovered the art of catching fish in waters that contain none" (Marx, *Capital*, p. 176) At the core of historical materialism is the simple but profound idea that people in order to continue living must produce food, clothing, shelter, new people, and so forth. The means by which they produce these necessities with their labor are in fact their means to life itself. Control of the means by which people produce is ultimately control of the people themselves. The particular form taken by the means of production varies according to the mode of production.

Means of Subsistence: All those things produced that are immediately consumed by humans. The means of subsistence are equal to the total product minus the sum of accumulation plus what enters into reproduction (raw materials and machinery). "Under *means of subsistence* is to be included *everything* which goes annually into the consumption fund. . ." (Letters, Marx to Engels, July 6, 1863).

Mechanical Materialism: Label applied to two fallacious currents of thought. Among Marxists it refers to those whose conception of materialism lacks a dialectical character, for example, to those who liquidate the role of consciousness and ideas in history. Mechanical materialism also characterizes the type of non-Marxian reasoning that views aspects of reality as radically separated and views their interaction in terms of strictly cause-and-effect models. It is materialist in the sense that it deals with here-and-now reality but mechanical in its conception of that object of focus.

Mediation: The action of an intervening agency. For example, Engels wrote that "as all action is *mediated* by thought, it appears to [people] to be ultimately *based* upon thought" (Letter to Franz Mehring, July 14, 1893). The reality is that material conditions (base) give rise to the need to think (mediation) out an action.

Mercantilism: Term coined by Adam Smith to characterize the period and policies followed by the West European and British nations from the sixteenth to the eighteenth centuries. The main feature of the period was that the state actively intervened in economic life by granting production and trading monopolies in order to insure a favorable balance of trade and accumulation of bullion. The mercantilist period is roughly equal to what Marx called the period of primitive accumulation.

Merchant Capital: Capital that is invested in purchasing goods in order to be able to resell them later at a higher price. The merchant capitalist seeks to buy cheap and sell dear.

Metaphysical Idealism: The belief that an external spiritual agency is the primary force accounting for human society and change. It is a characteristic of most religions. It is metaphysical because development is seen as mechanically caused by an outside agency rather than through the internal contradictions, processes, and changes of the thing itself. It is idealist because material reality, the social being of humans, is considered secondary in importance to spirit and ideas.

Metaphysics: In general use, the science that treats problems that transcend the sense world. *Metaphysical* is a term often used to describe religious world views. In Marxism, the term has a related but different use; it means the outlook that examines aspects of reality apart from their processes of change and interconnections with other aspects. There is a relationship between the Marxian and religious meanings, since the assumption that God is the cause of all changes in the world precludes the necessity of analyzing how those aspects change from their own internal developments.
See also LAW OF IDENTITY; MECHANICAL MATERIALISM; METAPHYSICAL IDEALISM.

Method: The disciplined way in which scientists investigate the objects of their study. Method includes both the premises of the study, e.g. the type of logic employed, and the techniques of research.
See also DIALECTICS; HISTORICAL MATERIALISM; METHOD OF PRESENTATION AND INQUIRY.

Method of Inquiry. *See* METHOD OF PRESENTATION AND INQUIRY.

Method of Presentation and Inquiry: Distinction made by Marx between the method used in the stage of investigation and the method used in reporting the results of the investigation.

> Of course the method of presentation must differ in form from that of inquiry. The latter has to appropriate the material in detail, to analyze its different forms of development, to trace out their inner connection. Only after this work is done, can the actual movement be adequately described. If this is done successfully, if the life of the subject-matter is ideally reflected as in a mirror, then it may appear as if we had before us a mere a priori construction. [Marx, *Capital*, p. 28]

Middle Class: In Marx's and Engels's writings, the bourgeoisie and petty bourgeoisie. *Bourgeoisie* and *upper middle class* were used synonymously, as were *petty bourgeoisie* and *lower middle class*. The upper middle class were the owners of large labor employing businesses while the lower middle class were small business owners, e.g., self-employed artisans, professionals, farmers, and shopkeepers. Marx and Engels adopted the common nineteenth-century use of the term *middle class*, the origin of which was the middle status position of the town bourgeoisie between the aristocracy and the peasantry in late feudalism. "I have used the word *Mittelklasse* all along in the sense of the English word middle-class (or middle-classes, as is said almost always). Like the French word bourgeoisie it means the possessing class, specifically that possessing class which is differentiated from the so-called aristocracy. . ." (Engels, *The Condition of the Working-Class in England*, p. 15). "The development of the middle class, the bourgeoisie, became incompatible with the maintenance of the feudal system. . ." (Engels, "Socialism: Utopian and Scientific," p. 103).

Mode of Distribution: Economic term for the complex of institutions that regulate the shares that individuals receive of the products of a society as a whole.
See also DISTRIBUTION.

Mode of Exchange: The way in which the products of labor are distributed. When Engels stated that "the mode of production is in rebellion against the mode of exchange" (*Anti-Duhring*, p. 327), he meant that the form of production is increasingly socialized cooperative labor, but the form in which the products of labor are distributed continues to be privatized, since the capitalist retains ownership.

Mode of Production: In general, the whole way a society produces. Human beings differ from animals in that they produce consciously, not instinctively. Consequently how people produce is what makes them distinctively human. The mode, or way, of production is both expansive in meaning and implication. In meaning it refers to all those ways in which human beings produce, including both the production of things and services and also the production of human beings themselves. Marx and Engels wrote in *The German Ideology*:

> This *mode of production* must not be considered simply as being the production of the physical existence of the individuals. Rather it is a definite form of activity of these individuals, a definite form of expressing their life, a definite *mode of life* on their part. As individuals express their life, so they are. What they are, therefore, coincides with their production, both with what they produce and with *how* they produce. [p. 37]

Marx and Engels analyzed the following historical modes of production: primitive communism, slavery, the Asiatic mode of production, feudalism, capitalism, and communism.
See also ASIATIC MODE OF PRODUCTION; CAPITALISM; COMMUNISM; FEUDALISM; PRIMITIVE COMMUNISM; SLAVE SOCIETIES—ANCIENT SOCIETY.

Moment: Hegelian term for each of the thesis and antithesis steps that contribute to the composition of the synthesis.
See also DIALECTICS; LAWS OF DIALECTICS; THESIS-ANTITHESIS-SYNTHESIS.

Monarchy: State form in which supreme power resides in one person. This person, the monarch, may receive the power through conquest, usurpation, election, or inheritance. The extent of the monarch's power may be limited by local nobles as was the case during much of European feudalism, or it may be "absolute" as was the case at different times from the fifteenth to the eighteenth centuries in England and France.
See also ABSOLUTISM.

Money: Commodity used as the measure of value and means to circulate other commodities. "The commodity that functions as a measure of value, and, either in its own person or by a representative, as the medium of circulation, is money" (Marx, *Capital*, p. 130).

Money and Real Capital: Distinction between actual capital as a self-expanding value and its representation in the various forms of money capital (stocks, bonds, promissory notes, credit, and so on). "The accumulation of the actual money-capital. To what extent is it, and to what extent is it not, an indication of an actual accumulation of capital, i.e., of reproduction on an extended scale?" (Marx, *Capital*, vol. 3, p. 476). The distinction between money and real capital is not a distinction between separate different types of capital; rather it is a distinction between levels of analysis, i.e., between the appearance and the essence of the movement of capital.

Money, Commodity, Industrial, and Productive Capital: Money and commodity capital have two applications in Marx's writings. First, money capital is simply capital in the form of cash or promissory notes, which can be invested, and commodity capital is capital in the form of commodities, which can be sold. Second, money, commodity, and productive capital together are categories that distinguish different steps in a production process that overall represents the functioning in industrial (as opposed to merchant's or moneylender's) capital. The first stage in the production process is the investment of money capital in purchasing means of production and labor power. In the second stage the industrial capital functions as productive capital when labor produces surplus value and reproduces value. In the third stage, that of the finished commodity, the industrial capital becomes commodity capital. The distinctions in Marx's words are as follows:

> The two forms assumed by capital-value at the various stages of its circulation are those of *money-capital* and *commodity-capital*. The form pertaining to the stage of production is that of *productive capital*. The capital which assumes these forms in the course of its total circuit and then discards them and in each of them performs the function corresponding to the particular form, is *industrial capital*, industrial here in the sense that it comprises every branch of industry run on a capitalist basis. Money-capital, commodity-capital, and productive capital do not therefore designate independent kinds of capital whose functions form the content of likewise independent branches of industry separate from one another. They denote here only special functional forms of industrial capital, which assumes all three of them one after the other. [*Capital*, vol. 2, p. 50]

Money-dealing Capital: Capital invested by the merchant in the technical aspects of tending money that is used to transform produced commodities into money, i.e., to sell produced commodities. Such technical aspects of money tending include bookkeeping, collecting, paying, and safekeeping. Money-dealing capital and commercial capital are the two forms of merchant's capital. (See Marx, *Capital*, vol. 3, chapter 19.)

Money Economy: Economy in which the majority of exchanges between producers and consumers are mediated through (involve the use of) money.

Money Form of Value: Type of exchange value equation analyzed by Marx in *Capital*, Chapter 1, Section 3 where the values of all commodities are expressed by how much of a single commodity set apart to which each is equivalent; the commodity set apart, i.e., the universal equivalent, is *money* which has the physical characteristics, i.e., its use value, that enable it to be used as a measure of value and means of circulation.
See ELEMENTARY FORM OF VALUE; EXCHANGE VALUE; EXPANDED FORM OF VALUE; GENERAL FORM OF VALUE; MONEY; RELATIVE AND EQUIVALENT FORMS OF VALUE; UNIVERSAL EQUIVALENT.

Moneylenders' Capital: Interest-bearing capital that is owned by those whose business it is to loan money to others for a specific period of time and rate of interest. Moneylenders' capital is the specifically capitalist form of interest-bearing capital as opposed to usurers' capital, which is the pre-capitalist form of interest-bearing capital in Marx's terminology.

Monism: The philosophical premise that the basis of existence derives from one source. There are materialist and idealist variants of monism, which respectively argue that the source of existence is either material or ideal reality.

Monogamy: Type of family based on sexual fidelity between one man and one woman.

Monopoly: Technically, a corporation that has total control of a particular market. American Telephone and Telegraph Company in the United States is an example of a monopoly. In Marxist writing the term *monopoly* is also used to cover oligopolistic situations, where a few companies dominate a particular market.

Mother-right: Projected period before the advent of private property, the monogamous family, and patriarchy where, according to Engels, family lineage was traced through the mother and she therefore had relatively more power. (See Engels, *The Origin of the Family, Private Property, and the State.*)

Motion: The process of change. "Motion in the most general sense, conceived as the mode of existence, the inherent attribute, of matter, comprehends all changes and processes occurring in the universe, from mere change of place right up to thinking" (Engels, *Dialectics of Nature*, p. 92).

Motion and Force: Force is a type of active motion that causes change. *Motion is the mode of existence of matter.* Never anywhere has there been matter without motion, nor can there be. . . . All rest, all equilibrium, is only relative, only has meaning in relation to one or other definite form of motion. . . . Matter without motion is just as inconceivable as motion without matter. Motion is therefore as uncreatable and indestructible as matter itself; as the older philosophy (Descartes) expressed it, the quantity of motion existing in the world is always the same. Motion therefore cannot be created; it can only be transferred. When motion is transferred from one body to another, it may be regarded, in so far as it transfers itself, is active, as the cause of motion, in so far as the latter is transferred, is passive. We call this active motion *force*, and the passive, the *manifestation of force.*

Hence it is as clear as daylight that a force is as great as its manifestation, because in fact the *same* motion takes place in both. [Engels, *Anti-Duhring*, p. 75]
See also FORCE.

Movable Capital. *See* NATURAL AND MOVABLE CAPITAL.

Mysticism: Concept that covers those types of thought that hold that true knowledge is inaccessible to the reasoning mind and that the means to true knowledge are through intuition or states of ecstasy.

N

Nation. *See* GENS, PHRATRY, TRIBE, NATION.

National Debt: The amount of claims which private creditors hold against a government in the form of bonds, pension rights, and so on. In the capitalist state the national debt tends to expand as state expenditures necessarily increase at a faster pace than sources of income. This dynamic increases the control of private capital (who are the creditors for new loans) over the state. "By what is the reversion of the state property to high finance conditioned? By the constantly growing indebtedness of the state. And the indebtedness of the state? By the constant excess of its expenditure over its income, a disproportion which is simultaneously the cause and effect of the system of state loans" (Marx, *Class Struggles in France, 1848-1850*, p. 112).

Natural and Movable Capital: Distinction between the *natural* form of capital, which evolved in workshops during feudal development and was kept rooted both in place and ownership; and the form of *movable* capital whose growth increased with the development of capitalism—i.e., those forms of capital (money, stocks, bonds, and commodities) that can be moved both from place to place and from owner to owner.
See ESTATE CAPITAL.

Natural Economy: Precapitalist economy characterized by production for direct use and consumption instead of for a market. Generally the greater part of a household's production was consumed by the household. In a natural economy the products of labor do not become commodities, and consequently the market does not mediate between production and consumption.

Nature and History Dialectic: The nature dialectic is the development of contradictions in nonhuman entities; the history dialectic is the development of contradictions through time in human relationships. A major debate exists in Marxism as to whether the two dialectics operate in essentially the same fashion. Those who answer in the negative argue that the history dialectic is qualitatively different because it involves consciousness.

Nature Dialectic. *See* NATURE AND HISTORY DIALECTIC.

Necessary and Surplus Labor: In Marxist political economy, necessary labor is the amount of labor required to produce the objects of consumption for the workers at their current level of consumption. Surplus labor is the amount of labor performed by workers that surpasses the amount of labor required to produce the objects of consumption for laborers at their current level of consumption. In other words, surplus labor is the amount of labor that surpasses necessary labor. Marx wrote in *Capital* (p. 209) that what distinguishes modes of production is the different manners in which surplus labor is extracted from the laborers.

Necessity. *See* FREEDOM.

Negation: Another term for antithesis.
See also DIALECTICS; LAWS OF DIALECTICS; THESIS-ANTITHESIS-SYNTHESIS.

Negation of the Negation. *See* LAWS OF DIALECTICS.

Neo-Kantianism. *See* KANTIANISM AND NEO-KANTIANISM.

Neo-Malthusianism. *See* MALTHUSIANISM AND NEO-MALTHUSIANISM.

Net Income: The difference between value realized and capital outlay. "The excess of the product (or the excess of its value) over that part of it which replaces the capital outlay, comprising both constant and variable capital" (Marx, *Theories of Surplus Value*, part 2, p. 547).

Nobility: Feudal social and legal class. The nobility were originally set apart as warriors from peasants and clergy. The original mainstay of the nobility were the knights, although in time a hierarchy of other internal class distinctions developed. They were granted land or other income-producing privileges in return for military services. The nobility developed its own mode of life and status consciousness which set it apart from social inferiors, over whom they also exercised authority. Beginning in the twelfth century the nobility developed from being only a *de facto* to also being a *de jure* superior class, i.e., their authority was legally ordained. This privileged legal position eventually became inheritable as the nobility consolidated their power. Engels used the term *nobility* loosely as a synonym for large landowners in the countries which were still feudalistic or semifeudalistic in his time. (See Engels, "On Social Relations in Russia.")

Nodal Point: Term used in dialectical logic for the point at which quantitative increase results in qualitative change.
See also LAWS OF DIALECTICS; THESIS-ANTITHESIS-SYNTHESIS.

Nominal and Real Wages: Distinction between the paper value of wages (nominal wages) and wages as measured against the amount of necessities that can be bought (real wages). "The sum of money which the laborer receives for his daily or weekly labor, forms the amount of his nominal wages, or of his wages estimated in value" (Marx, *Capital*, p. 508). Nominal wages are "the sum of money for which the worker sells himself to the capitalist" (Marx, "Wage Labour and Capital", p. 164). Real wages, on the other hand are "the sum of necessaries of life into which" the wages can be converted, "the sum of commodities which he can buy for" the nominal wages (ibid.). Marx introduced the distinction between nominal and real wages to analyze situations where, for example in inflation, one's nominal wages can go up while real wages go down. "Thus, the money price of labor, nominal wages, do not coincide with real wages, that is, with the sum of commodities which is actually given in exchange for the wages" (ibid.).
See also REAL AND RELATIVE WAGES.

Nominalism: The tendency in medieval scholastic philosophy that held that reality consists only of concrete particulars and consequently that intellectual general concepts have no independent existence—are not real. Marx and Engels rejected the complete position of nominalism but considered the stress on the primacy of concrete particulars to be one of the elements that contributed to the formation of modern materialism.

Nonantagonistic Contradiction. *See* CONTRADICTION.

Notion. *See* CONCEPT.

O

Object: Philosophical concept meaning that toward which consciousness is directed, those aspects external to the thinking mind.

Oppression: The resultant state of suffering caused by an unjust institution or authority. It is a general concept that includes particular examples, e.g., class, national, and sexual oppressions. In Marxism oppression includes but is not identical to the concept of exploitation, since the latter refers to a strictly economic process.

Organic Composition of Capital. *See* VALUE, TECHNICAL, AND ORGANIC COMPOSITIONS OF CAPITAL.

Overproduction Crisis: One of the classic forms of crisis in a boom-bust capitalist economy. During upswings in the business cycles production operates at a high level, but at some point the market becomes glutted. Then, since workers are not needed to produce more, they are laid off. Because the workers then do not have income to spend on buying the products, the crisis deepens.
See also CRISIS THEORY.

Ownership: Legal category for the resultant state of having purchased property.

P

Pairing Family: Marriage form that can be dissolved easily by either side. Engels described the form as "marriage between single pairs, with easy dissolution by either side" (*The Origin of the Family, Private Property, and the State*, p. 29). Engels inherited the term from the American anthropologist Lewis H. Morgan. In Morgan's writing the pairing family existed during the stage of barbarism.

Particular. *See* INDIVIDUAL, PARTICULAR, UNIVERSAL.

Patriarchal Family: Type of family in which a number of blood-related individuals is organized into a household under the domination of a male head.

Patricians: The members of the noble families of Rome. Senators, consuls, and pontifices came from patrician families.

Payments *in Kind*: Reimbursements made with a direct product (e.g., corn) instead of money.

Peasant Consciousness: The world view which theoretically corresponds to the peasant class position. The peasant way of life engenders individualism, a narrow perspective, and a respect for the sanctity of private property among certain of its sectors. Individualism is encouraged by the spatial isolation of the working conditions. The narrow perspective is encouraged by both the spatial isolation and the nonmarket character of much of production. The source of the private property respect is self-evident. Marx saw this respect as a major stumbling block to the development of an alliance with the proletariat. Nevertheless, he believed that the increasing economic strangulation of the peasantry by the capitalist farmers, state taxes, the urban money capitalists, all of which was sanctioned by an obliging judiciary, provided a basis for alliance with the working class. The continuing influence of the peasant consciousness is apparent in contemporary industrial conditions. In United States history, it has taken the form of the frontier as a safety valve for discontent; farming was a viable option for those who were unable to find satisfaction with industrial conditions. In the contemporary United States, the alienation among some youth has taken the form of a back-to-the-land movement and "five acres and independence" solutions to industrial and urban problems.

Peasants: Class that has day-to-day control over small patches of land (i.e., means of production) and whose work is directed chiefly toward the production of use values—not commodities. In non-Marxian general usage the term applies to anyone who does not own much property and lives and works on the land.

Penetration of Polar Opposites. *See* LAWS OF DIALECTICS.

Peonage: A form of slavery in which the individual has to bind over to a master control of his or her future labor power because of accumulated debts. Marx wrote in *Capital*, ". . . slavery is hidden under the form of *peonage*. By means of advances, repayable in labor, which are handed down from generation to generation, not only the individual laborer, but his family, become, *de facto*, the property of other persons and their families" (p. 165n).

Personal Property: Items owned by individuals or families that are used exclusively for direct consumption and not for income-producing purposes. Communism proposes the abolition of private ownership of income-producing property but not of personal property.

Petty Bourgeois Consciousness: The world view that theoretically corresponds to the petty bourgeois class position. The petty bourgeois class consciousness in any variation need not be articulated by members of the small business class themselves, but rather the consciousness may also be articulated by intellectual spokespersons for the class. Marx wrote in *The Eighteenth Brumaire of Louis Bonaparte* (p. 424) that what makes these intellectuals "representatives of the petty bourgeoisie is the fact that in their minds they do not get beyond the limits which the latter do not get beyond in life, that they are consequently driven, theoretically, to the same problems and solutions to which material interest and social position drive the latter practically." Classically, the components of petty bourgeois consciousness have grown out of the contradiction of, on the one hand, accepting the viability of capitalism as a small proprietor, and on the other, suffering the experience of being squeezed out of the market

by the big properietors. Marxists thus refer to this class as having a vacil-
lating character because although it can be expected to ally with the
working class to attack the excesses of big business, it will ally with
monopoly capital to defend the viability of capitalism.

> Thus, eternally tossing about between the hope of entering the ranks of the
> wealthier class, and the fear of being reduced to the state of proletarians or
> even paupers . . . possessed of small means, the insecurity of the possession
> of which is in the inverse ratio of the amount; this class is extremely vacil-
> lating in its views. Humble and crouchingly submissive under a powerful
> feudal or monarchical government, it turns to the side of Liberalism when
> the middle class is in the ascendent; it becomes seized with violent Demo-
> cratic fits as soon as the middle class has secured its own supremacy, but
> falls back into the abject despondency of fear as soon as the class below
> itself, the proletarians, attempt an independent movement. [Engels,
> "Revolution and Counter-Revolution in Germany" p. 304]

Petty bourgeois consciousness also embodies the individualism of the
classical capitalistic ethnic. Rather than achieving freedom through and
with the community, the small proprietor finds freedom in economic
independence from the community, in being her or his own boss. This
aspect of petty bourgeois consciousness appeals to some contemporary
workers precisely because they are trapped in the deadening alienation
and authoritarianism of the capital/labor relationship, where they are
anything but their own bosses.

Petty Bourgeoisie: Small business persons who do not significantly
employ wage or salaried labor. They own or control small shops, profes-
sional businesses, stores, farms, and so on, which are engaged in the
commodity market. Marx and Engels used the term *lower middle class* as
a synonym for the *petty bourgeoisie.*

Petty Bourgeois Socialism. *See* SOCIALISM, PETTY BOURGEOIS.

Phenomena: Kantian term for reality as it is *perceived* as opposed to the
way it actually is. The task of science is to pierce through the "phenom-
enal" to the essence of reality. In popular usage today *phenomena*
conveys a different meaning; it is a kind of catch-all phrase roughly
equivalent in meaning to *reality.*

Philistine: Pejorative term for people lacking in broad cultured interests
and bound by solely private, narrow, prosaic concerns.

Phratry: A social unit comprised of several gentes or clans. The concept

was used by the nineteenth-century American anthropologist Lewis H. Morgan who influenced Engels's work on the family.
See also GENS, PHRATRY, TRIBE, NATION.

Physiocrats: Eighteenth-century economic school whose main tenet was that land was the basis of wealth. Marx credited the leader of the physiocrats, Francois Quesnay, as having been the first to portray the circulation of economic life.

Piece and Time Wages: Different manners for calculating wages. Piece wages are calculated on the basis of the number of tasks the worker completes; time wages on the basis of the quantity of time the worker spends laboring.

Plebians: The nonslave common people of Rome. The term is sometimes used today to describe lower-class people.

Political Economy: Discipline that studies economic production and exchange.

> Political Economy, in the widest sense, is the science of the laws governing the production and exchange of the material means of subsistence in human society. Production and exchange are two different functions. Production may occur without exchange, but exchange—being necessarily an exchange of products—cannot occur without production. Each of these two social functions is subject to the action of special external influences which to a great extent are peculiar to it and for this reason each has, also to a great extent, its own special laws. But on the other hand, they constantly determine and influence each other. . . . The conditions under which men produce and exchange vary from country to country, and within each country again from generation to generation. Political economy, therefore, cannot be the same for all countries and for all historical epochs. . . . Political economy is therefore essentially a *historical* science. It deals with material which is historical, that is, constantly changing; it must first investigate the special laws of each individual stage in the evolution of production and exchange, and only when it has completed this investigation will it be able to establish the few quite general laws which hold good for production and exchange in general. At the same time it goes without saying that the laws which are valid for definite modes of production and forms of exchange hold good for all historical periods in which these modes of production and forms of exchange prevail. [Engels, *Anti-Duhring*, p. 177-78]

Polyandry: Marital system in which one woman can have more than one husband.

Polygamy: Marital system in which one man can have more than one wife.

Possession: Represents the right to consumption of an object by a particular person or group of persons. Unlike private property, possession does not necessarily assume private ownership; rather possession can ultimately assume socialized ownership or control of the object. Hence the right to determine who will consume particular objects in this latter case can be determined by the society as a whole rather than in accord with the dictates of individual exclusive ownership. "No ownership exists . . . before the family or the relations of master and servant are evolved, and these are much more concrete relations. It would, on the other hand, be correct to say that families and entire tribes exist which have as yet only *possessions* and not *property*" (Marx, Introduction to *A Contribution to the Critique of Political Economy*).

Practice: The act of actualizing theoretical knowledge and gathering new information to develop theoretical knowledge. Marx held that theory and practice were complementary steps in development.

Price: The empirical amount of money or amount in kind for which a commodity is bought or sold. Marx wrote, "*price*, taken by itself, is nothing but the *monetary expression of value*." ("Wages, Price and Profit", p. 53) However, actual prices may and usually do fluctuate above and below values.
See also PRICE AND VALUE THEORY.

Price and Value Theory: Distinction between levels of analysis in Marxist economic theory. Value theory deals with the relative amounts of social labor incorporated in different commodities; price theory deals with the actual empirical market prices of different commodities. Value theory is the underlying structure, which determines prices in the dialectical sense. Prices can, and most often do, fluctuate above and below the actual exchange value of a particular commodity. Values are to prices in economic theory as essences are to appearances (or manifestations) in dialectics.
See also LABOR THEORY OF VALUE.

Primitive Accumulation of Capital: Concept with two related meanings in Marx's writings. First, it refers to the historical precondition for a capitalist society: the laborers' means of production must be separated

from them and turned into capital, i.e., transformed from her or his own means of production to means of production owned by another who now confronts the laborer as an alien force. "The *primitive accumulation of capital* includes the centralization of the conditions of labor. It means that the conditions of labor acquire an independent existence in relation to the worker and to labor itself. This historical act is the historical genesis of capital, the *historical* process of separation which transforms the conditions of labor into capital and labor into wage-labor. This provides the basis for capitalist production" (Marx, *Theories of Surplus Value*, part 3, p. 314). Second, the primitive accumulation of capital refers to the actual amassing of wealth that could be transformed into capital from the plunder of the Americas, the slave trade, colonialism during the sixteenth and seventeenth centuries, and peasant expropriation, which went into the initial financing of European industrialization. "One of the most indispensable conditions for the formation of manufacturing industry was the accumulation of capital, facilitated by the discovery of America and the import of its precious metals" (Marx, *The Poverty of Philosophy*, p. 119).
See also ACCUMULATION OF CAPITAL.

Primitive Communism: The earliest mode of production. It was projected by Engels to be characterized by an absence of property ownership and class divisions. At the same time, though there was common posession of the means of production, there was an extremely low level of the force of production and hence little economic surplus.

Private Appropriation: Appropriation is to take into one's possession what was formerly not one's own. When Marx used the expression private appropriation, he was referring to the fact that within capitalist societies surplus value goes into the private possession of the capitalist to dispose of, rather than the social control of the society as a whole.
See also APPROPRIATION.

Private Property: Any income-producing object that is owned by one or more persons who have the exclusive right to its use so long as in doing so they do not violate the law.
See OWNERSHIP; PERSONAL PROPERTY; POSSESSION; PROPERTY

Production: The appropriation and fashioning by humans of the elements of nature for their own needs and uses. Production is a characteristic only of human beings. Engels wrote, "The essential difference between human and animal society is that animals are at most gatherers whilst men are *producers*'' (Letter to Lavrov, November 12, 1875). What makes production humanly defining is its fusing of creative intellectual conception of a task (unknown to animals) and execution. Production is thus a fundamental concept of Marxism.

See also COMMODITY PRODUCTION; COST OF PRODUCTION; CREATIVE LABOR; FORCES OF PRODUCTION; MEANS OF PRODUCTION; MODE OF PRODUCTION; RELATIONS OF PRODUCTION; REPRODUCTION; SOCIALIZATION OF PRODUCTION; SPHERE AND BRANCH OF PRODUCTION.

Productive and Individual Consumption: Distinction in uses of products. Productive consumption is the use of commodities as raw materials in a production process. They are productively consumed because in the act of their consumption a new product is created which incorporates the production of a new surplus value. Individual consumption is final consumption of products by private persons.

> Labor uses up its material factors, its subject and its instruments, consumes them, and is therefore a process of consumption. Such productive consumption is distinguished from individual consumption by this, that the latter uses up products, as means of subsistence for the living individual; the former, as means whereby alone, labor, the labor-power of the living individual, is enabled to act. The product, therefore of individual consumption, is the consumer himself; the result of productive consumption, is a product distinct from the consumer. [Marx, *Capital*, p. 179]

Productive Capital. *See* MONEY, COMMODITY, AND PRODUCTIVE CAPITAL.

Productive Labor: Labor that produces surplus value. Marx wrote that productive labor was "wage-labor which, exchanged against the variable part of capital (the part of the capital that is spent on wages), reproduces not only this part of the capital (for the value of its own labor-power), but in addition produces surplus-value for the capitalist." Conversely, unproductive labor is "labor which is not exchanged with capital, but directly with revenue, that is, with wages or profit. . . ." (Marx, *Theories of Surplus Value*, part 1, pp. 152-57).

Product of Labor: Any article produced by labor, whether for direct use of market exchange. All commodities are products of labor, but not all products of labor are commodities.

Profit: The empirical difference between the amount that a capitalist invests and what is received in a transaction. Profit can also be viewed as one of the parts into which surplus value is divided—the other two parts are rent and interest, according to Marx. *See also* FALLING RATE OF PROFIT; GENERAL RATE OF PROFIT; RATE AND MASS OF PROFIT; RATE OF PROFIT; SURPLUS PROFIT.

Proletarian Class Consciousness: The world view that theoretically corresponds to the working-class position and interests. Marx and Engels concluded that potentially proletarian class consciousness had as its content communism. They wrote, "It is not a question of what this or that proletarian, or even the whole proletariat, at the moment *regards* as its aim. It is a question of *what the proletariat is*, and what, in accordance with this *being*, it will historically be compelled to do" (*The Holy Family*, p. 44).
See also CLASS CONSCIOUSNESS; COMMUNISM; FALSE CONSCIOUSNESS; SOCIALISM.

Proletarian Internationalism: The Marxist dictum that class unity supercedes national unity in importance. "In the national struggles of the proletarians of the different countries, they [the Communists] point out and bring to the front *the common interests* of the entire proletariat, *independently of all nationality*" (Marx and Engels, "The Communist Manifesto" p. 120).

Proletariat. *See* WORKING CLASS.

Promiscuous Sexual Intercourse: Prefamily form of group marriage. According to Lewis H. Morgan, the American anthropologist on whose research Engels relied, the first stage after the evolution of humans from animals contained the feature of total group marriage, i.e., group sexual relations which did not exclude incest between ancestors and descendants or between brothers and sisters. (*See* Engels, *The Origin of the Family, Private Property and the State*, pp. 35-37.)

Property: Any object that is owned by one or more persons who have the exclusive right to its use so long as in doing so they do not violate the law. *See* OWNERSHIP; PERSONAL PROPERTY; POSSESSION; PRIVATE PROPERTY.

Punaluan Family: Form of group marriage that predated the modern nuclear family. According to Lewis H. Morgan, the American anthropologist on whose research Engels relied, the Punaluan family was the second stage of the family. It evolved out of the consanguine family, which in turn had evolved out of the original condition of promiscuous sexual intercourse. The Punaluan family form marked the final defeat of incest because within it sexual relations were forbidden between natural brothers and sisters as well as between ancestors and descendants as they had been in the consanguine family. In the punaluan group marriage a group of sisters were married in common to a group of men who were not their brothers, or conversely, a group of brothers married a group of women who were not their sisters. (See Engels, *The Origin of the Family, Private Property, and the State*, pp. 39-40.)

See also CONSANGUINE FAMILY; PROMISCUOUS SEXUAL INTERCOURSE.

Q

Qualitative Change. *See* LAWS OF DIALECTICS.

Quantitative Change. *See* LAWS OF DIALECTICS.

Quitrent: A payment in money or kind by the feudal peasant to the lord in lieu of performing services.

R

Rate and Mass of Profit: Distinctions in how profit is calculated. The rate of profit is equal to the quantity of surplus value produced divided by the sum of the invested variable and constant capital. The mass of profit is simply the gross quantity of profit produced. The distinction is important because the rate and mass of profit can vary in opposite directions.

Rate of Profit. *See* RATE AND MASS OF PROFIT.

Rate of Surplus Value: The amount of surplus value produced divided by the investment in labor power.

> *The rate of surplus* value, all other circumstances remaining the same, will depend on the proportion between the part of the working day necessary to reproduce the value of the laboring power and the *surplus time* or *surplus labor* performed for the capitalist. It will, therefore, depend on the ratio *in which the working day is prolonged over and above that extent,* by working which the working man would only reproduce the value of his laboring power, or replace his wages. [Marx, "Wages, Price and Profit," p. 58]

The rate of surplus value is also known as the rate of exploitation.

Raw Material: Marx distinguished between things spontaneously supplied by nature, which people simply gathered such as fish, water, and timber from a virgin forest, and materials taken from nature that already incorporate labor. In the former case in the act of, say fishing, labor is not working with a raw material; but if the already caught fish is being processed, then it is a raw material. In Marx's use, a raw material has to have already incorporated labor in its processing. These new materials are then the primary substances of production.

> Raw material may either form the principal substance of a product, or it may enter into its formation only as an accessory. An accessory may be consumed by the instruments of labor, as coal under a boiler, oil by a wheel, hay by draft-horses, or it may be mixed with the raw material in

order to produce some modification thereof, as chlorine into unbleached linen, coal with iron, dye-stuff with wool, or again, it may help to carry on the work itself, as in the case of the materials used for heating and lighting workshops. [Marx, *Capital*, p. 177]

See also MEANS OF PRODUCTION.

Reactionary: Political idea or stance whose result would be to roll back the positive developments of history to a preexisting state of affairs. Marx and Engels characterized as reactionary those political programs which would, consciously or unconsciously, reestablish feudal relations.

Real and Relative Wages: Distinction between the nominal value of wages and wages with respect to the rate of surplus value (*see* Rate of Surplus Value). Marx wrote, "real wages expressed the price of labor in relation to the price of other commodities; relative wages, on the other hand, express the share of direct labor in the new value it has created in relation to the share which falls to accumulated labor, to capital" ("Wage Labor and Capital," p. 164).
See also NOMINAL AND REAL WAGES.

Real Capital. *See* MONEY AND REAL CAPITAL.

Reality: The inner nature or essence of objects and thoughts. The inner nature is a composite of material and ideal factors, and the practical human activity which changes those factors. "The chief defect of all previous materialism . . . is that things, reality, sensuousness are conceived only in the form of the *object, or of contemplation*, but not as *sensuous human activity, practice*, not subjectively. . . . The dispute over the reality or non-reality of thinking which is isolated from practice is a purely *scholastic* question" (Marx, "Theses on Feurbach," p. 13).

Realization Crisis: Form of capitalist economic crisis that occurs when produced commodities cannot be sold. It is called a *realization* crisis because although surplus value has been produced, it cannot be realized or received by the capitalist.

Real Wages. *See* NOMINAL AND REAL WAGES; REAL AND RELATIVE WAGES.

Reason: In Hegelian philosophy the form of thought that reflects the Idea or divine purpose; it is thus the totality of universally valid principles. More generally reason is a concept associated with the French

Revolution that indicates that human beings have the faculty to understand and direct their lives.

Relation: The connection that one substance has to another. Since dialectics, in Engels' definition, is "the science of universal interconnection" (*Dialectics of Nature*, p. 27), the relation is the basic unit of analysis of that science. In a dialectical conception the relationship an aspect has with other aspects is a powerful determinant of the meaning of the aspect itself. Nothing exists in complete isolation. To be understood, it must be understood in its context or relationality. As opposed to isolated so-called facts, which are the units of analyses of bourgeois conceptions of science, Marxian science emphasizes relations as the units of analysis. The relation is the basic unit of analysis for a dialectical method. We cannot conceive of a society as a series of logically independent factors which are only externally related to each other, rather we must conceive of each factor as being both defined by its internal qualities and its relations to other factors. The core notion for any factor or category is itself a cluster of relations. Its meaning is defined by its relationships. (*See*, for example, Relations of Production) "The atom—formerly represented as the limit of divisibility—is now nothing more than a *relation . . .*" (Letters, Engels to Marx, June 16, 1867).

Relations of Production: Economic category that has as its object the structuring of how people interconnect in the work process of a particular mode of production. Relations of production thus extend from informal work norms to formalized legal system, such as in capitalism, which enforce the structuring of the interrelations of classes in a private-property system. Aside from what is given by nature such as air, the material conditions that enable human life to continue must be produced by the humans themselves. The instant that the production involves in one way or another the activity of more than one isolated individual, it becomes social. Social production *ipso facto* implies connections or relations among people. The term relation, a category from dialectics, expresses that what is important is the relationships between people over and above the isolated individual. Where the object of those relations is production, they are relations of production. Marx wrote in "Wage Labour and Capital" (p. 159) that "in production, men not only act on nature but also on one another. They produce only by cooperating in a certain way and mutually exchanging their activities. In order to produce, they enter into definite connections and relations with one another and only within these social connections and relations does their action on nature, does production, take place." Engels wrote,

What we understand by the economic relations, which we regard as the determining basis of the history of society, is the manner and method by which men in a given society produce their means of subsistence and exchange the products among themselves (in so far as division of labor exists.) Thus the *entire technique* of production and transport is here included. According to our conception this technique also determines the manner and method of exchange and, further, of the distribution of products and with it, after the dissolution of gentile society, also the division into classes, and hence the relations of lordship and servitude and with them the state, politics, law, etc. Further included in economic relations are the *geographical basis* on which they operate and those remnants of earlier stages of economic development which have actually been transmitted and have survived—often only through tradition or by force of inertia; also of course the external environment which surrounds this form of society. [*Letters*, Engels to W. Borgius, January 25, 1894]

Relative and Equivalent Forms of Value: Categories developed by Marx in *Capital*, Chapter 1, Section 3 for analyzing exchange value equations between commodities and the development from simple to complex forms of exchange. When one commodity is worth the same in exchange value as some other commodity, Marx calls the value of the former *relative* and the other *equivalent*. Relative value is the value of the original object of analysis while equivalent value is the value of that which it is measured against.

See also ELEMENTARY FORM OF VALUE; EXPANDED FORM OF VALUE; GENERAL FORM OF VALUE; MONEY; MONEY FORM OF VALUE; UNIVERSAL EQUIVALENT.

Relative Surplus Population. *See* SURPLUS POPULATION.

Relative Wages. *See* REAL AND RELATIVE WAGES.

Rent: In general the charge made for using property that is owned by another. Marx demonstrated in *Capital* that rent originates as a part of surplus value. Rent is one of the parts into which surplus value is divided —the other two are profit and interest.

See also CORVÉE; GROUND RENT; HOUSE RENT; QUITRENT; RENTIER.

Rentier: French term that originally meant the class of landlords who did not labor themselves but lived from rent received from their property. Today the term is sometimes used loosely to refer to all those who do no labor but receive income from the ownership of stocks and bonds.

Republic: One of the forms of the capitalist state. The defining feature of a republican form of state is that power is formally based in the people and their elected representatives as opposed to a monarchy where it is based in one person.

Reproduction: Concept used in a number of different senses in Marxist writing. Among them: (1) It refers to the activity of raising children. (2) It refers to the intergenerational production of the necessary ideological conditions for capitalist relations through socialization. (3) Institutions and activities are sometimes referred to as reproductive when their function is to provide indirectly the conditions necessary for the daily regeneration of labor power. For example, parks do not produce value but they may be necessary for the recreation of workers. (4) "Whatever the form of the process of production in a society, it must be a continuous process, must continue to go periodically through the same phases. A society can no more cease to produce than it can cease to consume. When viewed, therefore, as a connected whole, and as flowing on with incessant renewal, every social process of production is, at the same time, a process of reproduction" (Marx, *Capital* p. 531).

Reproduction on an Extended Scale. *See* SIMPLE REPRODUCTION AND REPRODUCTION ON AN EXTENDED SCALE.

Revenue: From the French *revenir*—to come back, meant in Marx's writing the personal income of the capitalist. Hence Marx distinguished that part of surplus value used for the personal income or "revenue" of the capitalist and that part reinvested or accumulated.

Revolution: Term with a philosophical and a social meaning in Marxism. Philosophically, a revolution is the movement in dialectics from the antithesis to the synthesis, i.e., the revolution is the negation of the negation. It is a "revolution" because the synthesis is now a new thesis constituted on a qualitatively new basis. The movement from antithesis to synthesis is revolutionary because it is a qualitative leap, a new threshold. Movement thus conceived of dialectically involves revolution. The social meaning of revolution flows from its philosophical-dialectical meaning. A social revolution is a qualitative change in the relations governing societal production, e.g., the change from feudalism to capitalism. In Marx's view the forces of production (antithesis) grow within the context of increasingly outdated relations of production (thesis). A social revolution is required to reestablish the relations of production in harmony with the forces of production (negation of the negation and synthesis). A social revolution in the Marxian sense is thus an uprising which replaces an outdated state form with a state form that allows for a new stage in economic development. The focus of the social revolution is the state form that institutionalizes the relations of production.

Revolutionary Situation: Time in which it is possible to effect a revolution. Marx and Engels wrote that if the

> material elements of a complete revolution are not present—namely, on the one hand the existing productive forces, on the other the formation of a revolutionary mass, which revolts not only against separate conditions of the existing society, but against the existing production of "life" itself, the "total activity" on which it was based—then it is absolutely immaterial for practical development whether the *idea* of this revolution has been expressed a hundred times already, as the history of communism proves. [*The German Ideology*, p. 62]

Marx wrote, "at a certain stage of development, the material productive forces of society come into conflict with the existing relations of production—or this merely expressed the same thing in legal terms—with the property relations within the framework of which they have operated hitherto. From forms of development of the productive forces these relations turn into their fetters. Then begins an era of social revolution" (Preface to *A Contribution to the Critique of Political Economy*, p. 21).

Role of Communists: To bring to the fore in all struggles of the working class their long-range interests as well as supporting the short-range interests.

> The Communists fight for the attainment of the immediate aims, for the enforcement of the momentary interests of the working class; but in the movement of the present, they also represent and take care of the future of that movement. . . . In short, the Communists everywhere support every revolutionary movement against the existing social and political order of things. In all these movements they bring to the front, as the leading question in each, the property question, no matter what its degree of development at the time. Finally, they labor everywhere for the union and agreement of the democratic parties of all countries. The Communists disdain to conceal their views and aims. They openly declare that their ends can be attained only by the forcible overthrow of all existing social condition." [Marx and Engels, "The Communist Manifesto," p. 136]

Ruling Class: The class that controls the state or in whose interest the state is operated in a particular country.

S

Savagery: Term used by Lewis H. Morgan, the nineteenth-century American anthropologist whose writings influenced Engels's theory of the development of the family. Savagery was the first stage after "the descent of man from the animal kingdom." It was "the period in which the appropriation of natural products, ready for use, predominated; the things produced by man were, in the main, instruments that facilitated this appropriation" (Engels, *The Origin of the Family, Private Property, and the State*, p. 28). In other words, savagery was primarily a gathering stage.

Scholasticism: Form of medieval Christian philosophy which deduced principles from religious dogma. It attempted to substantiate as theory and philosophy the Christian religious world view. Scholasticism was the philosophy of medieval (feudal) *Christian* society.

Science: The organized attempt to explain and accumulate knowledge about the universe. Science, from the Marxian point of view, is necessary to penetrate the phenomenon of things in order to uncover the essence. Science is thus a part of the creative relationship between people and their environment. Marx and Engels described science in general as "the expounding of the practical activity, of the practical process of development of men" (*The German Ideology*, p. 43).
See also ESSENCE AND APPEARANCE.

Scientific Law: Intellectual abstraction that portrays an essential relationship of the universe. The bourgeois conception of scientific law is that there are invariant causal relationships between varibles. Marx's and Engels's conception, to the contrary, introduced the dialectical concept of change such that all scientific laws are specific to particular historical stages of development. (*See* Historical Specification.) Hence, Engels wrote:

to us so-called "economic laws" are not eternal laws of nature but historical laws which arise and disappear; and the code of modern political economy, in so far as it has been drawn up with proper objectivity by the economists, is to us simply a summary of laws and conditions under which alone modern bourgeois society can exist—in short, the conditions of its production and exchange expressed in an abstract way and summarized. To us therefore none of these laws, in so far as it expresses *purely bourgeois relations*, is older than modern bourgeois society; those which have hitherto been more or less valid throughout all history really express only those relations which are common to the conditions of all society based on class rule and class exploitation. [Letter to F. A. Lange, March 29, 1865]

Sectarianism: Term originated historically with the development of Protestantism. (Similarly the term *dogmatism* originated historically with Catholicism.) A sect was a small group that separated from one or another of the main churches because it believed that the main church distorted or violated the pure doctrine. Within socialist and Communist movements a similar practice developed as a result of the way political disagreements were handled. The term sectarian in general then means the practice of forming small, isolated groups as opposed to working out disagreements within larger organized forms. Marx noted that "the development of socialist sectarianism and that of the real working-class movement always stand in inverse ratio to each other. Sects are justified (historically) so long as the working class is not yet ripe for an independent historical movement. As soon as it has attained this maturity all sects are essentially reactionary" (*Letters*, Marx to F. Bolte, November 23, 1871).

Self-estrangement of Labor: The state of the laborer in capitalism feeling apart from her or his own activity, which, instead of being an activity which develops humanly, dehumanizes and alienates.

Separation of Town and Country: Phrase in Marx's and Engels's writings that has several related meanings. (1) It refers to the historical process of populations dividing between those concentrated in cities and those scattered over the countryside. This process is consequence and cause of the economic division of labor between manufacturing and commerce in the towns and agriculture in the country. "The town is in actual fact already the concentration of the population, of the instruments of production, of capital, of pleasures, of needs, while the country demonstrates just the opposite fact, isolation and separation" (Marx and Engels, *The German Ideology*, p. 27). (2) Within the countryside and the cities, different class formations develop with differing interests, e.g., the interests of the industrial bourgeoisie versus the interests of the landed aristocracy. (3) The ways of life in both areas differ with progress, education, and the arts concentrated in the cities. This gives rise to a contradiction between the respective styles of life. (4) Inasmuch as the separation represents an antithetical movement dialectically (the division of unitary society), they will be rejoined at a higher level in a Communist society when the separation and contradictions will be overcome with a new synthesis (resolution) of the original contradiction.

Serfs and Free Peasants: Distinction between types of feudal dependency. Both feudal serfs and free peasants were bound to particular lords, i.e., a dependency contract was in force. In both cases the dependents owed rent or labor (the *corvée*) and services to the lord; in return the lord was the protector of the dependent in times of adversity. The difference between the two types of dependency was that the contract of free peasants ended whenever either they or the lord died. Thereafter the free peasant was theoretically free to choose any lord. The serf, on the other hand, was born into her or his contract, and it carried intergenerationally. The contract of the serf engaged both his person and his posterity to a lord's family line. Engels argued that in the latter stages of feudalism serfdom declined in favor or free peasant dependency. "The serfdom of the earlier Middle Ages, which still had in it much of ancient slavery, gave to the lords rights which lost more and more their value; it gradually vanished, the position of the serfs narrowed itself down to that of simple peasant tenants" (Engels, *The Peasant War in Germany*, p. 147).

Simple Reproduction and Reproduction on an Extended Scale: Stages in the productiveness of capital investments. Simple reproduction results from a production process which is able to produce a quantity equal to what is regularly consumed; reproduction on an extended scale results from production that incorporates growth, i.e., production that produces value greater than the original investment.

Slaves: Class of laborers who do not own the means of production and who do not own their own labor power. Their labor power is the preogative of another (the master) to use or sell.
See SLAVE SOCIETIES—ANCIENT SOCIETY.

Slave Societies—Ancient Society: Mode of production in which the main form of exploitation and production of wealth was based on slave labor —i.e., labor of human beings who are owned by others. Ancient Greece and Rome were the major Western examples of the slave mode of production. The American South before the Civil War was an example not of the slave mode of production but rather of slavery within the context of a capitalist mode of production.

Social: Adjective pertaining to any relationship between two or more persons, the composite of which is society.

Social Capital. *See* INDIVIDUAL AND SOCIAL CAPITAL.

Social Democratic Socialism. *See* SOCIALISM, SOCIAL DEMOCRATIC.

Socialism: General contemporary meaning, following Lenin-transitional form of society between capitalism and communism. As such, it is a mixed form containing both capitalistic and Communistic features. Capitalistic features (social classes, small-scale, income-producing property, and a repressive state apparatus) continue in ever diminishing respects in the context of such Communistic features as economic planning, redistribution of wealth, full employment, socialized medicine, and ideological education for the new society. Lenin's characterization of socialism as this transitional stage is derived from, but nevertheless different from, Marx and Engels's use of the term. Prior to 1848, Marx and Engels referred to socialism as a movement that was based in and made its appeal to middle classes. However, in Marx's last important writing, "The Critique of the Gotha Program," he distinguished between the lower and higher phases of Communist society. Marx's characterization of the lower phase corresponds to Lenin's and the contemporary use of the term socialism.
See also SOCIALISM, BOURGEOIS; SOCIALISM, CHRISTIAN; SOCIALISM, FEUDAL; SOCIALISM, PETTY BOURGEOIS; SOCIALISM, SOCIAL DEMOCRATIC; SOCIALISM, TRUE; SOCIALISM, UTOPIAN.

Socialism, Bourgeois: Tendency in socialist thought criticized by Marx and Engels, especially in "The Communist Manifesto." Bourgeois socialism essentially proposed to reform capitalism in the interest of the working class without doing away with the fundamental class and economic structure of capitalism. Liberal and social democratic thought would be the closest analogies today to bourgeois socialism.

Socialism, Christian (also called **Clerical Socialism**): Tendency in socialist thought criticized as reactionary by Marx and Engels, especially in "The Communist Manifesto." The Christian socialists of the 1840s in Europe patterned their movement after that of the early Christians whom they believed to have been Communistic. The Christian socialists longed for a return to a transformed precapitalist, preindustrial society rather than toward the future. Christian socialism was influential among many small artisans at the time Marx and Engels wrote "The Communist Manifesto." Among its most known spokespersons were Phillip Buchez and Hermann Wagener. Marx and Engels criticized Christian socialism because it sought to roll back history, proposed religion rather than science and internationalism as its basis, and because the essence of Christianity was not communism as was shown by the numerous infamies in history committed in its name.

Socialism, Feudal: Reactionary tendency in political and literary thought made up of representatives of the declining aristocracy who were critical of industrial capitalism. The feudal socialists proposed in mid-eighteenth century Europe to end the sufferings of the working class under capitalism by restoring the supposedly more harmonious society of the Middle Ages. Marx and Engels in "The Communist Manifesto" criticized feudal socialism. Among the representatives of feudal socialist thought were a section of the French Legitimists—backers of the overthrown Bourbon dynasty in 1830; Young England (c. 1830-1845)—a group of aristocratic offspring active in the debates over electoral law reform; and the writer Thomas Carlyle.

Socialism, Petty Bourgeois: Tendency in socialist thought criticized as reactionary by Marx and Engels, especially in "The Communist Manifesto." The base of petty bourgeois socialism exists in countries with a large number of independent peasants and proprietors. The petty bourgeois socialists were highly critical of industrial capitalist society. They proposed to reintroduce the guild system of independent artisans in manufacturing and to increase the number of peasant proprietors in agriculture as the solution to the evils of capitalism. The Swiss economist Jean Charles Leonard Dismond de Sismondi (1773-1842) was the leading representative of what Marx and Engels characterized as petty bourgeois socialism. They characterized it as reactionary because it proposed a roll back of history.

> In its positive aims, however, this form of Socialism aspires either to restoring the old means of production and of exchange, and with them the old property relations, and the old society, or to cramping the modern means of production and of exchange, within the framework of the old property relations that have been, and were bound to be, exploded by those means. In either case, it is both reactionary and Utopian. [Marx and Engels, "The Communist Manifesto," p. 130]

Socialism, Social Democratic: Type of socialism characterized by a mixed economy (i.e., capitalist and socialist) and the maintenance of classes. The state intervenes actively in economic and social planning as well as sponsoring welfare programs. Social democratic socialism is not seen as a transition to communism nor is there a dictatorship of the proletariat form of state as in Marxian socialism. "The peculiar character of the Social-Democracy is epitomised in the fact that democratic-republican institutions are demanded as a means, not of doing away with two extremes, capital and wage labor, but of weakening their antagonism and transforming it into harmony" (Marx, *The Eighteenth Brumaire of Louis Bonaparte*, p. 423).

Socialism, True: Movement of radical German intellectuals in the 1840s. Moses Hess was the chief theoretician. Others included Karl Grun, Otto Luning, and Karl Heinzen. The true socialists, heavily influenced by Feuerbach, based their views on abstract moral principles of justice and an abstract human nature. These abstractions were to be the measure of any social system. Like the utopian socialists, the true socialists appealed to the moral superiority of socialism. Marx and Engels attacked true socialism, especially in "The Communist Manifesto," on two grounds. First, based on classless moral arguments and an abstracted ahistorical notion of human nature, the true socialists neglected to analyze and base their political program on the specific economic position of the working class. Second, politically the true socialists adopted an ultraradical stance of not allying with the bourgeoisie to bring down German absolutism. They delivered the main blow of their criticism against the rising bourgeoisie rather than the nobility who were in power. Hence Marx and Engels concluded that their brand of socialism served the interests of the feudal reaction.

Socialism, Utopian: Nineteenth-century socialist movement mainly associated with Robert Owen, Hentir Saint Simon, and Charles Fourier. Marx and Engels referred to it as *utopian* socialism because its proponents appealed only to the moral superiority and desirability of socialism rather than demonstrating scientifically that socialism was a historical stage which out of necessity would follow capitalism.

Socialization of Production: Refers to the increasing division of labor and interdependency of production units which accompanies the growth of industrialization. The tendency is for any given commodity to incorporate the coordinated labor of large numbers of workers. For example, a can of beer incorporates the labor of—to mention only a few—farmers, millers, miners, aluminum workers, paint workers, brewery workers, and transportation workers. The increasing socialization of production is one of the material preconditions for the establishment of socialism.

Socially Necessary Labor Time: Average amount of time required to complete a task given current standards of average labor productivity. Marx wrote, "the labor-time socially necessary is that required to produce an article under the normal conditions of production, and with the average degree of skill and intensity prevalent at the time" (*Capital*, p. 47). Marx introduced the concept of socially necessary labor time to qualify the labor theory of value in order to avoid the absurd conclusion that a lazy or unskilled laborer who took more time to do a task than a proficient laborer would thereby produce more value.
See also LABOR THEORY OF VALUE; SOCIAL LABOR.

Social Labor: Abstract concept of average labor productivity which is used for calculating exchange value production. Average productivity is determined by the average amount of time required to perform a given task in a particular industry in a society. Hence, for example, there is an average length of time among mechanics required to rebuild a particular type of carburetor. It is this average of quantity of social labor which goes into the calculation of the amount of exchange value produced.

Social Revolution. *See* REVOLUTION.

Socioeconomic Formation (sometimes written simply as **form**): An empirically existing constellation of social or economic arrangements in history as opposed to a theoretical construct. For example capitalist *mode of production* is a theoretical abstraction to which no actual societies fully conform. Actual societies are socioeconomic formations which may have the characteristics of more than one mode of production. For example, the pre-Civil War United States was a socioeconomic formation characterized by elements of the feudal and slave as well as the predominating capitalist mode of production.

Solipsism: The philosophy that *I* alone exist and that all objective reality, even other people, have no independent existences—they are creations of *my* consciousness or created only for my world.

Sophistry: The act of using intentionally specious or fallacious arguments in order to deceive, display ingenuity, or simply win an argument. The term originated as a critical characterization of the Greek Sophist school of philosophy.

Species-being: Universal characteristics that distinguish humans as a species. "Species-being" is generally equivalent to the contemporary concept of human nature. Marx inherited the concept "species-being" from Ludwig Feuerbach (German philosopher, 1804-1872). Feuerbach and Marx included in their concept of "species-being" the conclusion that humans are beings who can have consciousness of their essential nature as a species—as opposed to each one only knowing her or his own individual needs. Marx posited two general aspects to the essential nature of human beings. (1) Humans are social beings, i.e., their essential natures are determined by their interrelations with others. "The human essence is no abstraction inherent in each single individual. In its reality it is the ensemble of the social relations" (Marx, "Theses on Feuerbach," p. 14). (2) Humans develop themselves as humans through *creative* labor, whereas the labor of animals is instinctual. Engels stated the point as follows: "The essential difference between human and animal society consists in the fact that animals at most *collect* while men *produce*" (*Letters*, Engels to P.L. Lavrov, November 12, 17, 1875). Beyond these general humanly defining characteristics which can be alienated, e.g. in class societies, human beings are variable.
See also BEING; CREATIVE LABOR.

Speculation: Capitalist investment practice. Normal investments realize surplus value through gaining control of new production facilities and using them. Speculative investments, on the other hand, gain profits not by using the new property for production but rather by selling it at a later date for a higher price. The speculator invests on the probability that the price of a property or security will rise. If many investors bid on the property or in the same market, then demand forces rises in prices above exchange values. Speculation is based on prices being in excess of values.
See also PRICE AND VALUE THEORY.

Speculative Philosophy: Types of philosophy that derive propositions about reality not from experience but from logical thought. Speculative philosophy is a method consistent with some forms of idealism. Hegel, for example, examined through deduction according to dialectical logic the development of ideas. Other speculative philosophers were Descartes and Fichte.
See also IDEALISM; MATERIALISM.

Sphere and Branch of Production: Classification devices for types of production. Sphere of production is a category for the different general areas of production, e.g., industry, mining, agriculture, and so on.

Branch of production is the particular type of production within a sphere of production, e.g., the cotton industry.

Spiral Form of Development: Descriptive term for the way history develops that is contained in the third law of dialectics (the negation of the negation). It states that history is developmental as opposed to cyclical or linear.
See also LAWS OF DIALECTICS.

Spirit: Idealist Hegelian concept described by Marx and Engels as follows: "*Hegel's* conception of history presupposes an *Abstract* or *Absolute Spirit* which develops in such a way that mankind is a mere *mass* that bears the Spirit with a varying degree of consciousness or unconsciousness. Within *empirical*, exoteric history, therefore, Hegel makes a *speculative*, esoteric history, develop. The history of mankind becomes the history of the *Abstract Spirit* of mankind, hence a *spirit far removed* from the real man" (*The Holy Family*, p. 100). Spirit generally means self-consciousness of the Idea or moving force of history which is God's will. Religious thought assumes that God (spirit) created the world. Spirit for religion also has a second reference. The soul of a person, that is, that part of a person's being which is seen as the spiritual as distinct from the physical side. It is through the soul that God, the spirit, presumably directs the human world.

Stagnant Relative Surplus Population. *See* SURPLUS POPULATION.

State: "The state is the form in which the individuals of a ruling class assert their common interests and in which the whole civil society of an epoch is epitomised" (Marx and Engels, *The German Ideology*, p. 99). The Marxist definition of the state thus emphasized the class content of state rule. The state exists because there is an exploited class to be subjugated and an exploiting class whose property must be protected. Marx also emphasized as a part of his concept the ideologies that stabilize and legitimize the existence of a particular state. Engels in *The Origin of the Family, Private Property, and the State* categorized the three major historical forms of the state according to the three major forms of exploitation: There has been a slave state, feudal state, and capitalist state. "The state is nothing but the organized collective power of the possessing classes, the landowners and the capitalists, as against the exploited classes, the peasants and the workers" (Engels, "The Housing Question," p. 347). Marx and Engels wrote that the bourgeois state "is nothing more than the form of organization which the bourgeois

are compelled to adopt, both for internal and external purposes, for the mutual guarantee of their property and interests" (*The German Ideology*, p. 99).
See also BONAPARTISM; DICTATORSHIP OF THE PROLETARIAT; MONARCHY; REPUBLIC.

State Capital: Capital that is used by governments to employ labor directly or indirectly through the contracting of the work to private firms. The general source of state capital is taxation.

Structure: Refers to two levels of analysis in Marxist writing. First, it refers to the concrete relations of production as they are manifested in definite institutions and legal systems. Second, it refers to how the various aspects of the totality of a mode of production interrelate with each other toward the result of maintaining that mode of production.

Subject: Philosophical concept for the thinking mind. Subject is counterposed to the object which is what the thinking mind perceives.

Subject of Labor: That which labor is working on in order to transform. For example, in wooden chair making the subject of labor would be the wood. The subject of labor is one of the three elementary parts of a labor process. "The elementary factors of the labor-process are 1, that personal activity of man, i.e., work itself, 2, the subject of that work, and 3, its instruments" (Marx, *Capital*, p. 174).

Sublate: English word used to render the meaning of the German *aufheben* ("to raise up"). In dialectical logic it means that the resolution of a contradiction both negates the previous stage of the contradiction but also incorporates the truthful aspects of the contradiction in a higher stage of development.
See also DIALECTICS, LAWS OF DIALECTICS.

Superstructure: The legal, political, ideological, and cultural systems that reflect the economic structure of a society. Superstructure is an architectural concept and analogy introduced by Marx to emphasize that legal and political systems do not develop autonomously. Rather, their development is related to a greater or lesser degree to developments within the economic structure of society.
See STRUCTURE; TOTALITY.

Supply and Demand Theory: Theory that prices on the market are determined by the relation between the supply and demand for a particular commodity. If there is a high supply but low demand, prices will fall. If there is a high demand, but short supply, they will rise. Supply and demand theory is considered by Marxists to be superficial and ideological when taken alone in the absence of a theory of value as an explanation of market price differences. It is ideological to the extent that it fosters the notion that shrewd business practices on the part of the capitalist account for the creation of profit and that consumers do have democratic control over the economy since allegedly it is their demand which accounts for price changes. However, Marxists do grant that supply and demand theory can be useful to explain price oscillations above and below the true *values* of commodities if interpreted within the context of the labor theory of value.

Surplus Labor. *See* NECESSARY AND SURPLUS LABOR.

Surplus Population: Concept developed by Marx to explain the creation in capitalist societies of a part of the labor force that was underemployed or unemployed. Marx wrote in *Capital* (p. 590) that "with the growth of the total capital, its variable constituent or the labor incorporated in it, also does increase, but in a constantly diminishing proportion." The result is the production of a "relatively redundant population of laborers, i.e., a population of greater extent than suffices for the average needs of the self-expansion of capital, and therefore a surplus-population." These workers are surplus, not in any Malthusian sense of an absolute over-population, but in the sense that they are not needed on a full-time basis in a capitalist economy. Their labor cannot be utilized profitably by the capitalist. In a socialist economy, freed from the dictates of profit, there would be no necessity to keep part of the labor force idle. Marx also used the concept of a surplus population in his studies of France to describe that part of the bourgeoisie who were no longer needed to manage their capital actively and who either became the idle rich or who sought out positions in the state. In the early stages of capitalism the surplus population is made up of those who have been driven off the land and for whom there is insufficient employment in the cities. After industrialization, they are made up of workers displaced by machinery. Engels also mentions as members of the surplus population those capitalists who no longer manage capital but simply are coupon clippers living off dividends, interest, and stock manipulations carried out by their agents. ("Socialism: Utopian and Scientific", p. 145).

> The capitalist has no further social function than that of pocketing dividends, tearing off coupons, and gambling on the Stock Exchange, where the different capitalists despoil one another of their capital. At first the capitalistic mode of production forces out the workers. Now it forces out

the capitalists, and reduces them, just as it reduced the workers, to the ranks of the surplus population, although not immediately into those of the industrial reserve army. [Ibid.]

Another source of membership into the surplus population is the continual pressures that drive small business under. Marx wrote, "small-holding property . . . produces an unemployed surplus population for which there is no place either on the land or in the towns, and which accordingly reaches out for state offices as a sort of respectable alms, and provokes the creation of state posts" (*The Eighteenth Brumaire of Louis Bonaparte*, p. 482).

Marx termed a part of the surplus population as the *relative* surplus population. They are that part of the surplus population who in Marx's day were shifted in and out of jobs in accordance with the shifts in the business cycle and who functioned to regulate accumulation. The permanently unemployed and the rentiers are members of the surplus population but not members of the relative surplus population. The industrial reserve army is another term for the relative surplus population. Marx analyzed three forms of the relative surplus population.

First, the *floating* form is that part of the relative surplus population which lives in the centers of industry, i.e., the industrial cities, who are employed and unemployed according to the needs of capital. In upswings of the business cycle they find jobs, but during downswings they are discharged.

Second, the *latent* form refers to the underemployed or irregularly employed agricultural laborers. Their condition arose because the relative amount of labor needed in agriculture diminishes with capitalist and technological development. Eventually they will be forced to move to the industrial areas.

Third, the *stagnant* form refers to the irregularly employed part of the relative surplus population whose jobs, when they get them, are significantly below the average in working conditions. Unlike the floating relative surplus population who move between normal working-class jobs according to the needs of capital, the stagnant surplus population move among the worst jobs.

Surplus Product: "The portion of the product that represents the surplus-value" (Marx, *Capital*, p. 220). In other words, the surplus product is that part of the product which is equivalent in value to the difference between the value of what labor produces and the value of what is expended in production.

See also EXCHANGE VALUE; SURPLUS VALUE.

Surplus Profit: Profit above the average rate due to above average business conditions. Surplus profit exists "in every sphere of industrial production for any capital which is put to work under conditions better than the average" (*Letters*, Marx to Engels, August 2, 1862).

Surplus Value: Marxist economic concept explainable in three different ways. First, at every stage of production of commodities the workers involved reproduce the value of the investment in means of production and labor power and create an additional exchange value. This additional value is surplus value. In other words, the final exchange value of a commodity less the value of the invested capital in means of production and labor power equals the surplus value. Second, the difference between the exchange value of labor power and the value of labor, that is, what labor produces, equals surplus value. The worker is thus paid the value of her or his labor power but not the full value of what her or his labor produces. The value of the labor power, like that of any commodity, is set by the labor which goes into its production. Third, Marx also formulated the same basic equation in terms of the time involved. The working day can be divided between that portion of the day when the worker reproduces the value invested by the capitalist in means of production and labor power and that portion of the day when the worker produces exchange value beyond what was invested. Marx called the first part of the day necessary labor and the second part surplus labor. The difference between the time of the working day and necessary labor equals surplus value. Exploitation in the Marxist sense means precisely the appropriation by the capitalist class of the surplus value produced by the working class. Surplus value production and expansion is the driving force of the capitalist political economy.

Synthesis. *See* THESIS-ANTITHESIS-SYNTHESIS.

Systems of Consanguinity: The various patterns of familial relationships that exist to tie together blood relatives.

T

Tautology: "The simple repetition in the predicate of what is already expressed in the subject" (Engels, *Anti-Duhring*, p. 55). A tautology is a type of reasoning error which can occur in many areas of knowledge production. The producer produces a pseudo-product. He or she states as a proof, definition, or other conclusion that which was the originating problem, only in different words. Nothing new is added.

Technical Composition of Capital. *See* VALUE, TECHNICAL, AND ORGANIC COMPOSITIONS OF CAPITAL.

Technological Determinism: The view that the development of technology (knowledge of the techniques of production) is the motive force of history. This view is often mistakenly attributed to Marx. Marx, to the contrary, viewed technology as only one part of the overall forces of production which propel historical development.
See also FORCES OF PRODUCTION.

Technology: From the Greek *logos* or knowledge of techniques, in particular knowledge of the techniques of production. In Marxism technology means the progressive development of knowledge of the techniques which exand and increase the productivity of labor. Technology is considered to be one of the complex of forces of production which contribute to economic development.
See also FORCES OF PRODUCTION.

Teleology: The study of final ends which supposedly evidence purpose or design in nature. Teleology is the view that all components of reality have a purpose. Some schools of philosophy see that purpose as beyond the ability of people to comprehend and only in the realm of God; others see the purpose as being the task of philosophy to discover. Teleological tenets exist in the works of Aristotle and Hegel.

Tendency: Category used to describe a probabilistic or hypothetical direction of a process of development. For example, Marx concluded that there is a tendency for the rate of profit to decline as the organic composition of capital increases. A tendency specifies a probabilistic not an absolute prediction.

Theory: A systematic explanation of the patterns of interrelationships among aspects of reality. Social theory is a systematic explanation of the patterns of interrelationships among social events, processes, and formations. Marxist theory is composed of concepts and tendencies which focus on what is essential in an object of investigation.
See also CONCEPT; ESSENCE AND APPEARANCE; TENDENCY.

Thesis-Antithesis-Synthesis (the **Triad**): Formulation of dialectical development where there is first a thesis stage in a process. A contradiction, or antithesis, with the thesis develops. The thesis and the antithesis struggle. The resolution of the contradiction is the synthesis, which itself is the thesis of a new stage of development.
See also LAWS OF DIALECTICS.

Time Wages. *See* PIECE AND TIME WAGES.

Total Ground Rent. *See* GROUND RENT.

Total Form of Value. *See* EXPANDED FORM OF VALUE.

Totality: Concept of dialectics that social reality is interrelated and that this interrelationship constitutes a whole or totality which affects each of the parts within. The totality defines the meaning of each of the internal parts. The totality is a sociohistorical process, since the whole is always changing and developing.
See also DIALECTICS.

Transformation Problem, the: The largely unresolved task in Marxian economics of developing a theory to account for the gap between economic values and prices of particular commodities.
See also PRICE AND VALUE THEORY.

Transition Class: Classes which either originate in and cohere with a previous mode of production, e.g., peasants and landlords in capitalism, or are viable only in the first stages of the contemporary mode of production, e.g., the petty bourgeoisie in capitalism. Transition classes lose their economic footing progressively as the mode of production develops.

Triad. *See* LAWS OF DIALECTICS; THESIS-ANTITHESIS-SYNTHESIS.

Tribe: Originally, a community of people united by common blood descent. In later historical periods tribes were based on people who lived and whose ancestors had lived in a common territory, regardless of blood relationship.
See also GENS, PHRATRY, TRIBE, NATION.

True Socialism. *See* SOCIALISM, TRUE.

Trust: Combination of all companies in a single field under the same management. Engels wrote:

> This led in some branches, where the scale of production permitted, to the concentration of the entire production of that branch of industry in one big joint-stock company under single management. This has been repeatedly effected in America; in Europe the biggest example so far is the United Alkali Trust, which has brought all British alkali production into the hands of a single business firm. The former owners of the more than thirty individual plants have received shares for the appraised value of their entire establishments, totalling about 5 million pounds, which represent the fixed capital of the trust. The technical control is concentrated in the hands of the general management. [Comment to Marx's text in *Capital*, vol. 3, p. 438]

"The producers on a large scale in a particular branch of industry in a particular country unite in a 'Trust,' a union for the purpose of regulating production. They determine the total amount to be produced, parcel it out among themselves, and thus enforce the selling price fixed beforehand" (Engels, *Anti-Duhring*, p. 328).

Truth: The valid reflection in thought of its object.

> But precisely therein lay the true significance and the revolutionary character of the Hegelian philosophy . . . that it once for all dealt the death blow the finality of all products of human thought and action. Truth, the cognition of which is the business of philosophy, was in the hands of Hegel no longer an aggregate of finished dogmatic statements, which, once discovered, had merely to be learned by heart. Truth lay now in the process of cognition itself, in the long historical development of science, which mounts from lower to ever higher levels of knowledge without ever reaching, by discovering so-called absolute truth, a point at which it can proceed no further, where it would have nothing more to do than to fold its hands and gaze and wonder at the absolute truth to which it had attained. And what holds good for the realm of philosophical knowledge holds good also for that of every other kind of knowledge and also for practical action. [Engels, *Ludwig Feuerbach and the End of Classical German Philosophy*, p. 339]

"Man must prove the truth, i.e., the reality and power, the this-worldliness of his thinking in practice" (Marx, "Theses on Feuerbach," p. 13).

U

Universal. *See* INDIVIDUAL, PARTICULAR, UNIVERSAL.

Universal Equivalent: Marxian economic term for that commodity that has the particular characteristic that through it all other commodities can be related to each other. The commodity which has that characteristic and plays that role is *money*.

Unproductive Labor. *See* PRODUCTIVE LABOR.

Upper Middle Class. *See* CAPITALIST CLASS; MIDDLE CLASS.

Use Value: The purpose which an object has for consumption. Use value is hence a qualitative measure. In contrast to exchange value which is the measure which capitalist development employs, use value is the measure which guides Communist and most socialist development.

Usufruct: The feudal right of peasants to use the common lands for gathering wood, grazing cattle, and so on. One of the factors that undermined the peasant's economic position in the early stages of capitalist development was the withdrawal of the usufruct. The classic case was England where the Enclosure Acts denied peasants use of the common lands.

Usurer's Capital: Precapitalist form of capital. A usurer was a person in the Middle Ages who loaned out money at an exorbitant rate of interest in spite of the Catholic church's disapproval. Usurer's capital was thus a form of interest-bearing capital that predated the beginnings of the capitalist mode of production. "Interest-bearing capital, or, as we may call it in its antiquated form, usurer's capital, belongs together with its twin brother, merchant's capital, to the antediluvian forms of capital, which long precede the capitalist mode of production and are to be found in the most diverse economic formations of society" (Marx, *Capital*, vol. 3, p. 593). "What distinguishes interest-bearing capital—in so far as it is an essential element of the capitalist mode of production—from usurer's capital is by no means the nature or character of this capital itself. It is merely the altered conditions under which it operates, and consequently also the totally transformed character of the borrower who confronts the money-lender'' (ibid., p. 600).

Utilitarianism: The view originally formulated by Jeremy Bentham that the usefulness of any practical action can be evaluated by calculating mathematically the amount of resulting pleasure and suffering. Utilitarians believed that individuals were motivated by what they would individually get in terms of pleasure out of particular actions and that public policy ought to attempt to maximize the greatest amount of pleasure for the greatest possible amount of people. Marx and Engels analyzed utilitarianism to be a world view that originated from bourgeois and petty bourgeois social relations (e.g., egoism and exploitation).

> The complete subordination of all existing relations to the relation of utility, and its unconditional elevation to the sole content of all other relations, occurs for the first time in Bentham's works, where, after the French Revolution and the development of large-scale industry, the bourgeoisie is no longer presented as a special class, but as the class whose conditions of existence are those of the whole society. . . . The economic content gradually turned the utility theory into a mere apologia for the existing state of affairs, an attempt to prove that under existing conditions the mutual relations of people are the most advantageous and generally useful. [Marx and Engels, *The German Ideology*, pp. 436-438]

Utopian Socialism. *See* SOCIALISM, UTOPIAN.

V

Value. *See* EXCHANGE VALUE; PRICE AND VALUE THEORY; USE VALUE; LABOR THEORY OF VALUE; SURPLUS VALUE; ABSOLUTE AND RELATIVE SURPLUS VALUE; RELATIVE AND EQUIVALENT FORMS OF VALUE; RATE OF SURPLUS VALUE.

Value of Labor: The economic value that labor creates. Marx distinguished this from the value of labor power or wages.

Value of Labor Power: The exchange value of the commodity of physical and/or mental capacity to work (labor power) which the capitalist purchases from the worker. Marx argued that the value of the commodity of labor power, given the labor theory of value, was set like that of any other commodity: "Like that of every other commodity, its value is determined by the quantity of labor necessary to produce it. . . . After what has been said, it will be seen that the *value of laboring power* is determined by the *value of the necessaries* required to produce, develop, maintain, and perpetuate the laboring power" ("Wages, Price and Profit," p. 56).

Value, Technical, and Organic Composition of Capital: Different measures of the relative amounts of means of production versus labor power employed in a particular production process. The value composition of capital expresses the amount of capital in exchange value terms which is invested in the means of production versus that which is invested in labor power. The value composition of capital is thus "the proportion in which (capital) is divided into constant capital or value of the means of production, and variable capital or value of labor-power, the sum total of wages" (*Capital*, p. 574). The technical composition of capital is an empirical measure of the actual amount of means of production used in a production process in relation to the amount of labor necessary to operate those means of production. The technical composition of capital is thus "the relation between the [physical] mass of the means of production employed [in the production process], on the one hand, and the mass of labor necessary for their employment on the other'' (ibid.). Between the technical and value compositions of capital there is a relationship although it is not always a one to one relationship. Marx called the value composition of capital the organic composition of capital to the extent that it mirrored changes in the technical composition of capital. The organic composition of capital is thus a measure of changes over time in the ratio of means of production to labor power in a particular production process. Between the technical and value compositions of capital ''there is a strict correlation. To express this I call the value-composition of capital, in so far as it is determined by its technical composition and mirrors the changes of the latter, the *organic composition of capital*'' (ibid.). The value and technical compositions of capital are measures of the relationship between means of production and labor power at one point in time; the organic composition of capital is a measure of changes in that relationship over time.

Value Theory. *See* PRICE AND VALUE THEORY.

Variable Capital. *See* CONSTANT AND VARIABLE CAPITAL.

Vassalage: The system of personal dependence among the upper classes of feudalism. A subordinate (e.g., a knight) swore loyalty, including availability for military service, to a superior (i.e., the lord) in return for protection and often the means for a livelihood, e.g., a grant of land. Vassalage was one part of the massive ties of personal relations which bound together the feudal social structure.
See also SERFS AND FREE PEASANTS.

W

Wages: What the worker receives in return for the sale of her or his labor power to the capitalist. In contemporary economics a distinction is made between wages and salaries. Wages are paid by the hour whereas salaries are paid by the week, month, or year. Both wages and salaries, though, are included under the original Marxist meaning of wages. Wages are "the equivalent with which the capitalist buys the temporary disposal of labor-power" (Marx, part I of *Theories of Surplus Value*, p. 86).

Way of Life. *See* MODE OF PRODUCTION.

Will: The composite of interests and desires that a person or persons have which they seek to attain.

Working Class: Those who do not own the means of production and therefore have to sell their labor power in order to earn a livelihood. Engels defined the working class as "the class of modern wage-laborers who, having no means of production of their own, are reduced to selling their labor-power in order to live" ("The Communist Manifesto," p. 108n). In Marx's and Engels's writings, proletariat was used as a synonym for the working class. ". . . the *proletarian* i.e., the man, who, being without capital and rent, lives purely by labor, and by a one-sided, abstract labor . . ." (Marx, *Economic and Philosophic Manuscripts of 1844*, p. 31). Aside from the main stratum of the working class, Marx and Engels analyzed as other strata the labor aristocracy and the surplus population.
See LABOR ARISTOCRACY; LUMPENPROLETARIAT; SURPLUS POPULATION.

World Market. *See* MARKET.

X Y Z

Zadruga: South-Slavic form of the patriarchal household community which predated the modern nuclear family. In the patriarchal household community several generations, under the leadership of a male—the patriarch—shared the same household, worked the land collectively, and shared in common the produce. Engels wrote that the patriarchal household community "constituted the transition stage between the mother-right family which evolved out of group marriage and the individual family known to the modern world. This appears to be proved at least as far as the civilized peoples of the Old World, the Syrians and Semites, are concerned" (*The Origin of the Family, Private Property, and the State*, p. 58). The Zadruga was, according to Engels, "the best existing example of such a family community." He described it as follows:

> It embraces several generations of the descendants of the father and their wives, who all live together in one household, till their fields in common, feed and clothe themselves from the common store and communally own all surplus products. The community is under the supreme management of the master of the house (*domacin*), who represents it in external affairs, may dispose of smaller objects, and manages the finances, being responsible for the latter as well as for the regular conduct of business. He is elected and does not by any means need to be the eldest. The women and their work are under the direction of the mistress of the house (*domacica*), who is usually the *domacin's* wife. In the choice of husbands for the girls she has an important, often the decisive voice. Supreme power, however, is vested in the Family Council, the assembly of all adult members, women as well as men. To this assembly the master of the house renders his account; it makes all the important decisions, administers justice among the members, decides on purchases and sales of any importance, especially of landed property, etc." [Ibid., p. 59]

APPENDIX

TERMS GROUPED
BY SUBJECT AREA

POLITICAL ECONOMY

Absolute and Relative Surplus Value
Accumulation of Capital
Alienation
Amortization
Anarchy of Capitalist Production
Auxiliary Materials
Bank Note
Barter
Bill of Exchange
Capital
Cartel
Centralization of Capital
Circulation of Capital
Circulation of Commodities
Commerce
Commercial Bourgeoisie
Commercial Capital
Commodity
Commodity Market
Commodity Production
Concentration of Capital
Concrete and Abstract Labor
Constant and Variable Capital
Consumption
Cooperative Labor
Cost of Production
Cost-Price
Credit
Credit Capital
Crisis Theory
Discounting
Distribution
Division of Labor

Economic Structure of Society
Economic Surplus
Elementary Factors of the Labor Process
Estate Capital
Exchange
Exchange Value
Expanded Form of Value
Exploitation
Expropriation
Extractive Industries
Falling Rate of Profit
Fictitious Capital
Financial Aristocracy
Fixed and Circulating Capital
Forces of Production
Free Labor
Fundamental Contradiction of Capitalism
General Form of Value
General Law of Capitalist Accumulation
General (Average) Rate of Profit and Surplus Profit
Gross Income
Ground Rent
Husbandry
Individual and Social Capital
Instruments of Labor
Interest
Interest-bearing Capital
Joint-stock Company
Labor
Labor Market
Labor Power
Labor Theory of Value
Laborer
Land Capital
Landlord Class
Living and Dead Labor
Machine
Market
Market Price
Means of Production
Means of Subsistence
Merchant Capital
Mode of Distribution
Mode of Exchange
Mode of Production

Money
Money and Real Capital
Money, Commodity, Industrial, and Productive Capital
Money-dealing Capital
Money Economy
Money Form of Value
Moneylenders' Capital
Monopoly
National Debt
Natural and Movable Capital
Natural Economy
Necessary and Surplus Labor
Net Income
Nominal and Real Wages
Overproduction Crisis
Payments in kind
Peonage
Piece and Time Wages
Political Economy
Price
Price and Value Theory
Primitive Accumulation of Capital
Productive and Individual Consumption
Productive Labor
Product of Labor
Profit
Property
Rate and Mass of Profit
Rate of Surplus Value
Raw Material
Real and Relative Wages
Realization Crisis
Relations of Production
Relative and Equivalent Forms of Value
Rent
Reproduction
Revenue
Scientific Law
Simple Reproduction and Reproduction on an Extended Scale
Socialization of Production
Socially Necessary Labor Time
Social Labor
Speculation
Sphere and Branch of Production
State Capital
Subject of Labor

Supply and Demand Theory
Surplus Product
Surplus Profit
Surplus Value
Technology
Transformation Problem
Trust
Universal Equivalent
Use Value
Usurers' Capital
Value
Value of Labor
Value of Labor Power
Value, Technical, and Organic Compositions of Capital
Wages

SOCIOLOGY-ANTHROPOLOGY

Alienation
Apprentice
Asiatic Mode of Production
Aristocracy
Barbarism
Benefice
Bourgeois Consciousness
Bureaucracy
Capitalism
Capitalist Class
Civilization
Civil Society
Class
Class Consciousness
Class Struggle
Commercial Bourgeoisie
Communism
Consanguine Family
Consciousness
Corvée
Craft
Creative Labor
Division of Labor
Economic Structure of Society
Economic Surplus
Endogamy
Estate
Exogamy

False Consciousness
Family
Feudalism
Fief
Financial Aristocracy
Freedom
Gens (plural Gentes)
Gens, Phratry, Tribe, Nation
Gentile Constitution
Goal of Capitalism
Group Marriage
Guild
Hetaerism
Ideology
Industrial Bourgeoisie
Industrial Reserve Army
Intercourse
Journeyman
Labor
Labor Aristocracy
Laborer
Lumpenproletariat
Manager
Master
Middle Class
Mode of Production
Money Economy
Monogamy
Mother-Right
Nation
Natural Economy
Nobility
Oppression
Pairing Family
Patriarchal Family
Peasant Consciousness
Peasants
Peonage
Petty Bourgeois Consciousness
Petty Bourgeoisie
Phratry
Polyandry
Polygamy
Primitive Communism
Production
Proletarian Class Consciousness

Promiscuous Sexual Intercourse
Punaluan Family
Rentier
Reproduction
Ruling Class
Savagery
Scientific Law
Self-Estrangement of Labor
Separation of Town and Country
Serfs and Free Peasants
Slaves
Slave Societies—Ancient Society
Species Being
Surplus Population
Systems of Consanguinity
Technology
Transition Class
Tribe
Usufruct
Vassalage
Working Class
Zadruga

SOCIAL PSYCHOLOGY

Alienation
Bourgeois Consciousness
Class Consciousness
Consciousness
Creative Labor
False Consciousness
Fetishism
Ideology
Oppression
Peasant Consciousness
Petty Bourgeois Consciousness
Proletarian Class Consciousness
Self-Estrangement of Labor
Species Being
Will

GENERAL PHILOSOPHY

Agnosticism
Antinomy

A Priorism
Asceticism
Atheism
Being
Critique
Definition
Deism
Dualism
Eclecticism
Economic Determinism
Empiricism
Hypothesis
The Idea
Idealism
Immanent
Individual, Particular, Universal
Kantianism and Neo-Kantianism
Law of Identity
Mechanical Materialism
Metaphysics
Metaphysical Idealism
Monism
Mysticism
Nominalism
Object
Phenomena
Scholasticism
Solipsism
Sophistry
Speculative Philosophy
Spirit
Subject
Tautology
Teleology
Utilitarianism
Will

MARXIAN METHOD, DIALECTICS

Abstraction
Being
Contradiction
Category
Definition
Determination

Dialectics
Dialectical Idealism
Dialectical Materialism
Essence and Appearance
Fetishism
Freedom
Historical Materialism
Historical Specification
In Itself and For Itself
Individual, Particular, Universal
Labor
Laws of Dialectics
Manifestation
Material Conditions of Life
Materialism
Matter
Method
Method of Presentation and Inquiry
Moment
Motion and Force
Nature and History Dialectic
Negation
Nodal Point
Practice
Reality
Reason
Relation
Science
Scientific Law
Spiral Form of Development
Structure
Sublate
Superstructure
Tendency
Theory
Thesis-Antithesis-Synthesis
Totality
Truth

POLITICS, POLITICAL SCIENCE, STATE ANALYSIS

Absolutism
Anarchism
Bonapartism
Bourgeois Right
Bureaucracy

Colony
Counterrevolution
Coup d'état
Dictatorship of the Proletariat
Dogmatism
Economism
Factionalism
Gentile Constitution
Ideology
Monarchy
Nation
National Debt
Practice
Proletarian Internationalism
Republic
Reactionary
Revolution
Role of Communists
Ruling Class
Sectarianism
Socialism
Socialism, Bourgeois
Socialism, Christian
Socialism, Feudal
Socialism, Petty Bourgeois
Socialism, Social Democratic
Socialism, True
Socialism, Utopian
State Capital

LEGAL

Appropriation
Bourgeois Right
Gentile Constitution
Law
Ownership
Possession
Private Appropriation
Private Property
Property

HISTORY, MISC.

Corn Laws
Corvée

Enclosure Acts
Fief
Guild
Hetaerism
History
Industrial Revolution
Journeyman
Malthusianism and Neo-Malthusianism
Master
Mercantilism
Mother-Right
Nobility
Patricians
Philistine
Physiocrats
Plebians
Quitrent

FEUDALISM

Apprentice
Benefice
Corvée
Craft
Enclosure Acts
Estate
Estate Capital
Feudalism
Guild
Journeyman
Landlord Class
Master
Monarchy
Nobility
Peasants
Peonage
Quitrent
Serfs and Free Peasants
Usufruct
Usurers' Capital

SELECTED
BIBLIOGRAPHY

REFERENCES CITED

Engels, Frederick. 1878 [1969]. *Anti-Duhring: Herr Eugen Duhring's Revolution in Science*. Moscow: Progress.

_____. 1845 [1973]. *The Condition of the Working-Class in England. Moscow:* Progress.

_____. 1882 [1954]. *Dialectics of Nature*. Moscow: Foreign Languages Publishing House.

_____. 1872 [1970]. "The Housing Question," in Marx and Engels, *Selected Works in Three Volumes*. Moscow: Progress.

_____. 1888 [1970]. *Ludwig Feuerbach and the End of Classical German Philosophy*. Ibid.

_____. 1894 [1970]. "On Social Relations in Russia." Ibid.

_____. 1884 [1948]. *The Origin of the Family, Private Property, and the State*. Moscow: Progress.

_____. 1850 [1965]. *The Peasant War in Germany*. Moscow: Progress.

_____. 1852 [1972]. "Revolution and Counter-Revolution in Germany" in Marx and Engels, *Selected Works in Three Volumes*. Moscow: Progress.

_____. 1880 [1970]. "Socialism: Utopian and Scientific." Ibid.

_____. 1883 [1970]. "Speech at the Graveside of Karl Marx." Ibid.

Hegel, G. W. F. 1807 [1967]. *The Phenomenology of Mind*. New York: Harper & Row.

_____. 1837 [1953]. *Reason in History*. New York: Bobbs-Merrill.

Marx, Karl. 1867 [n.d.]. *Capital*, Volume 1. Moscow: Progress.

_____. 1861-1877 [1971]. *Capital*, Volume 2. Moscow: Progress.

_____. 1865 [1971]. *Capital*, Volume 3. Moscow: Progress.

_____. 1850 [1970]. *The Class Struggles in France 1848 to 1850*, in Marx and Engels, *Selected Works in Three Volumes*. Moscow: Progress.

_____. 1859 [1970]. *A Contribution to the Critique of Political Economy*. Moscow: Progress.

_____. 1875 [1970]. "Critique of the Gotha Program," in Marx and Engels, *Selected Works in Three Volumes*. Moscow: Progress.

_____. 1844 [1959]. *Economic and Philosophic Manuscripts of 1844*. Moscow: Progress.

_____. 1846 [1955] *The Poverty of Philosophy*. Moscow: Progress.

_____. 1863 [1968]. *Theories of Surplus Value*, 3 Parts. Moscow: Progress.

_____. 1845 [1970]. "Theses on Feuerbach," in Marx and Engels, *Selected Works in Three Volumes*. Moscow: Progress.

_____. 1849 [1970]. "Wage Labour and Capital," Ibid.

_____. 1865 [1970]. "Wages, Price, and Profit." Ibid.

Marx, Karl and Frederick Engels. 1846 [1976]. *The German Ideology*. Moscow: Progress.

_____. 1844 [1975]. *The Holy Family, or Critique of Critical Criticism*. Moscow: Progress.

_____. 1848 [1970]. *The Communist Manifesto*. In Marx and Engels, *Selected Works in Three Volumes*. Moscow: Progress.

_____. 1953. *Selected Correspondence*. Moscow: Foreign Languages Publishing House.

_____. 1970. *Selected Works in Three Volumes*. Moscow: Progress.

OTHER REFERENCES

Bloch, Marc. 1940 [1961]. *Feudal Society*, 2 vol. Chicago, Illinois: University of Chicago Press.

The Compact Edition of the Oxford English Dictionary. Oxford: Oxford University Press, 1971.

Dowd, Douglas F. 1974. *The Twisted Dream: Capitalist Development in the United States Since 1776*. Cambridge: Winthrop.

Gerth, Hans, and C. Wright Mills. 1953. *Character and Social Structure*. New York: Harcourt, Brace and Company.

Goldmann, Lucien. 1969. *The Human Sciences & Philosophy*. London: Grossman.

Gransci, Antonio. 1957. *The Modern Prince & Other Writings*. New York: International.

Lenin, V. I. 1970. *Selected Works in Three Volumes*. Moscow: Progress.

Lukács, Georg. 1922 [1971]. *History and Class Consciousness: Studies in Marxist Dialectics*. London: Merlin.

_____. 1925. "Technology and Human Relations," in Lukács, *Marxism and Human Relations* 1973.

_____. 1973. *Marxism and Human Relations*, ed., E. San Juan, Jr. New York: Dell.

Manfred, A. Z., ed. 1974. *A Short History of the World*. Moscow: Progress.

Nicolaievsky, Boris, and Otto Maenchen-Helfen. 1936 [1976]. *Karl Marx: Man and Fighter*. London: Penguin.

Remmling, Gunter W. 1967. *Road to Suspicion: A Study of Modern Mentality and the Sociology of Knowledge*. New York: Appleton, Century, Crofts.

Ryazanoff, David. 1922 [1972]. *The Communist Manifesto of K. Marx and F. Engels*. Calcutta: Radical Book Club.

Selsam, H. 1949. *Handbook of Philosophy*, ed. and adapted from the *Short Philosophic Dictionary* by M. Rosenthal and P. Yudin. Proletarian Publishers.

Stace, W. T. 1924 [1955]. *The Philosophy of Hegel*. New York: Dover.

Williams, Raymond. 1976. *Keywords: A Vocabulary of Culture and Society*. New York: Oxford.

About the Author

JAMES RUSSELL studied at the University of Wisconsin. He has taught at San Francisco State University and is now assistant professor of Sociology at the University of Texas at El Paso. His articles have appeared in *Science & Society*, *Politics and Society*, and *Radical America*.

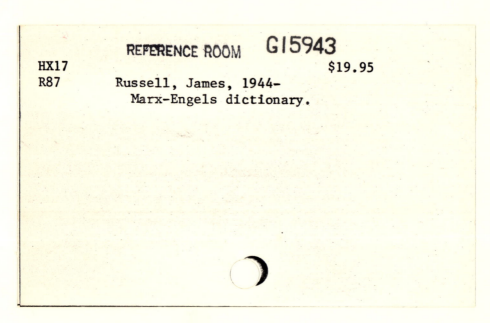